D1552549

Amazing Conversions

Amazing Conversions,

WHY SOME TURN TO FAITH & OTHERS ABANDON RELIGION

Bob Altemeyer & Bruce Hunsberger

Ⓟ Prometheus Books
59 John Glenn Drive
Amherst, New York 14228-2197

Published 1997 by Prometheus Books

01 00 99 98 97   5 4 3 2 1

Library of Congress Cataloging-in-Publication Data

Altemeyer, Bob, 1940–
    Amazing conversions : why some turn to faith and others abandon religion /
Bob Altemeyer and Bruce Hunsberger.
        p.   cm.
    Includes bibliographical references.
    ISBN 1–57392–147–5 (cloth : alk. paper)
    1. Conversion—Psychological aspects. 2. Atheism—Psychological aspects.
3. Converts—Canada—Psychology—Case studies. 4. Atheists—Canada—
Psychology—Case studies. 5. Christian education   —Psychology.
I. Hunsberger, Bruce. II. Title.
    BR110.A48   1997
    291.4′2—dc21   97–3301
                                                                CIP

Contents

Acknowledgments

This book exists because some amazing people were willing to share the stories of their lives with the authors, who will always be grateful to them.

Susan Alisat helped Hunsberger by typing the transcripts of the Wilfrid Laurier University interviews. Altemeyer would not let anyone help him do anything.

Prometheus Books has been a pleasure to work with. In particular, the authors thank Paul Kurtz for his enthusiasm for this book, and his dedication to "finding the truth, whatever it is." Eugene O'Connor was a helpful and joyfully tolerant editor who let the authors tell the story precisely as they wished.

Bob Altemeyer would like to dedicate this book to Chris Argyris, whom he had as a "prof" at Yale thirty-six years ago. Chris led him to realize he really had no idea who he was or why he was determined to become a rich businessman. If psychology has suffered as a result, he certainly profited.

Bruce Hunsberger never did want to become a rich businessman, and he had no similar pivotal undergraduate experience. However, if Bob Altemeyer had not been his Ph.D. supervisor, this book and Hunsberger's research program would not exist, and his life would be much less interesting. Consequently, he would like to dedicate this book to Bob.

1

Normal People

I believe in one God, the Father almighty, maker of heaven and earth, and of all things visible and invisible. And in one Lord Jesus Christ, the only-begotten Son of God. Born of the Father before all ages, God of God, light of light, true God of true God. Begotten not made; being of one substance with the Father; by whom all things were made. Who for us men, and for our salvation, came down from heaven. And was incarnate by the Holy Ghost of the virgin Mary: and was made man. He was crucified also for us, suffered under Pontius Pilate, and was buried. And the third day He rose again according to the Scriptures. And ascended into heaven. He sitteth at the right hand of the Father. And he shall come again with glory to judge both the living and the dead; of whose kingdom there shall be no end. And I believe in the Holy Ghost, the Lord and giver of life: Who proceedeth from the Father and the Son. Who together with the Father and the Son is adored and glorified. Who spoke by the Prophets. And in one, holy, catholic

9

and apostolic Church. I confess one baptism for the remis-
sion of sins. And I look for the resurrection of the dead.
And the life of the world to come. Amen.

This is popularly known as the Nicene Creed. It dates back to the fourth century C.E., and for over 1,600 years it has summarized the basic beliefs of Christianity. One of the authors of this book memorized this creed when he was growing up. Maybe you did, too.

How much of it do you believe? All of it? Some? None?

Here is a tougher question: Why? Whatever you believe, *why* do you believe it? Why don't you believe something else?

Your answer probably begins with your upbringing, with what you were taught as a child. For most people, that decides things. We acquire our religion from our parents almost as certainly as we inherit the color of our eyes. For example, in a recent study of nearly two thousand students at the University of Manitoba and Wilfrid Laurier University, 97 percent of the Catholics had been raised in Catholicism, 97 percent of the Jews had grown up in Judaism, and 96 percent of the Protestants had been brought up Protestants—usually in their present denomination, in fact.*

What about atheists and agnostics, people who belong to no religion, not even generic Christianity? Only 47 percent of the "Nones" had been brought up that way, outside religion. Where did the other half of the "nonbelievers" come from, then? They were *apostates*, persons who had given up the

---

*The scientific support and references for facts asserted in this book will be found in the notes at the end of each chapter. For example, details of this study, to which we shall often refer, will be found in note 1 to this chapter.[1] In general, we shall banish the technical reporting and terms to these notes, as this book is written for general readers interested in religion.

religion in which they had been raised. They had become the "lost sheep" Jesus spoke of in Matthew 18.

What led the apostate students astray? Was it their atheistic college professors? Sex and drugs? Rock-and-roll?

Well, we can absolve their professors, because these students were studied at the very beginning of their freshman year. They *arrived* on campus as apostates. Was it earlier sex, drugs, and rock-and-roll then? These may have played a role in some cases, but the "key factor" lay elsewhere.

You can make a pretty good prediction of how much a university student, raised as a Christian, will still accept Christianity if you know how much the family religion was emphasized while he was growing up. For example, in the study under discussion, about 80 percent of the students raised Christians said they were still Christians, while the other 20 percent were now "nothing." The biggest difference we could find between these two groups appeared in how much the home religion had been stressed. Parents of those who had "kept the faith" emphasized religion *twice* as much as the parents of those who had become apostates.[2]

(So if today's young people seem less religious than their parents, it may be traced to their parents' neglecting to pass on the grandparents' training. In a study of over five hundred students and their parents, the parents said they received stronger religious training from *their* folks—i.e., the grandparents—than their children reported receiving from them.[3])

The overall finding that you shall reap what you sow will not surprise many. Religions undoubtedly appreciated the generalization eons ago, for they have long stressed spiritual education of their young. Whatever their official position on free will, all the major Christian sects bet heavily on determinism when it comes to the next generation's religious decisions. And you can see that bet pays off; one can strongly influence adults' religious choices through childhood training. Nearly all of the students in our study stayed in the family religion, especially if it had been stressed during their youth.

But we would bet, in turn, that many parish priests and ministers know "exceptions to the rule." That is, there are individuals whose childhoods were rich with religion emphasis, but who nonetheless abandoned their faith when they became adults, to become "nothing." The other exceptions pop up as well: persons who had practically no religious instruction at all, and yet as adults became deeply religious out of very "stony soil." How can one explain these anomalies?

This book hopes to provide some explanation of these two exceptional kinds of persons: individuals who—against the influences of their past and all the socialization theories in the world—swam against the tide and became, respectively, "Amazing Apostates" and "Amazing Believers." It presents our research on rare persons who changed so mightily that they "crossed over" and became each other's destiny. It tries to understand how such remarkable transformations could take place.

QUESTIONS AND DOUBTS

Before we deal with the exceptional cases, however, let's develop a little "background" by seeing what *usually* happens. Whether people have been raised in a religion or not, questions about the existence of God, evil, and an afterlife often arise in childhood. We have found that university students say they wondered about such things as early as age three. But for most students, the questions arise during adolescence—typically between twelve and fourteen. What sort of issues come up?

Questions about Religion

In the fall of 1995, we asked our nearly two thousand students how often questions about religious matters had arisen in their minds. You will probably get a better "feel" for their answers if you respond to the items yourself. Please note: We are not asking whether the questions were resolved or not. Rather, to what extent did *questions* about these issues ever come up in your mind? (Simply ignore the numbers in parentheses after each item, for now.)

0 = Not at all
1 = Slightly
2 = Somewhat
3 = Moderately
4 = Quite
5 = Very
6 = Extremely

1. The existence of God, an all-good, all-powerful supreme being who created the universe. (3.16) (2.08)

2. The problem of evil and unfair suffering in the world. (3.33) (2.37)

3. The history of religion; bad things religions did in the past. (2.20) (1.87)

4. Evolution vs. Creation. (3.25) (2.40)

5. The way religious people sometimes pressured others to believe what they believe. (3.30) (2.54)

6. The hypocrisy of "religious" people (i.e., the nonreligious behavior of supposedly religious people). (3.18) (2.49)

7. Getting to know people from other religions, or people with no religion. (2.33) (1.37)

8. The death of a loved one. (3.51) (2.01)

9. Religious teachings about sex. (2.20) (1.91)

10. The way some religious people seemed interested mainly in getting money from others. (2.58) (2.28)

11. The intolerance some religious people showed toward other religions. (3.23) (2.59)

12. Religious teachings about the role of women. (2.56) (2.33)

13. Threats about what would happen if you were bad (e.g., being condemned to hell). (2.49) (1.93)

14. Finding that being religious did not bring peace and joy after all. (1.69) (1.63)

15. The intolerance some religious people showed toward certain other people (e.g., homosexuals). (3.24) (2.64)

16. Claims that the Bible is the word of God. (2.23) (1.84)

17. The way religion kept people from enjoying themselves in sensible ways. (2.19) (1.90)

18. Religious teachings often did not make sense; they seemed contradictory or unbelievable. (2.30) (2.07)

19. What happens to us when we die; is there really an after-life? (3.84) (2.47)

20. Religious faith made people "blind," not questioning teachings that should be questioned. (2.33) (2.13)

The first number in parentheses after each item shows the average rating for that question. So number 19 ("What happens to us when we die; is there really an afterlife?") had been the biggest question in these students' past (3.84, on a 0–6 range). In contrast, few questioned religion because (no. 14) "being religious did not bring them peace and joy after all." Its mean equalled only 1.69.

You can see that, overall, questions arose "moderately" often (i.e., about a "3" on our scale). Some people reported wondering a lot; others, hardly at all. Was the degree of past religious emphasis related to this? No. Such questions came up at least as often in the minds of students from highly religious backgrounds as among students with virtually no religious training.

Doubts about Religion

However, questions do not necessarily lead to *doubts*, to a mistrust of religious teachings. They may be answered satisfactorily, or overwhelmed by other religious experiences. The individual may simply "drop" them. So we asked the students to go through the list again, and say how much they now *doubted* the value of religion because of each issue. (You might like to do so, too.)

The second number in parentheses after each item shows the strength of these doubts, on average. You will immediately notice, if you compare each pair of numbers, that *questions* were often resolved. (That is, the second number is always lower than the first.) Overall these university students were hardly afire with religious doubts, the average being about "2" ("Somewhat").

Looking more closely, we can see that religions handled questions about the existence of God (no. 1), the problem of evil (no. 2), and death (nos. 8 and 19) rather well. These "scores" dropped more than any others. On the other hand, people who had trouble finding peace and joy in being religious (no. 14), or who felt that religious teachings often did not make sense (no. 18), or that faith made one blind (no. 20) were seldom reassured. These scores dropped least.

Looking at the "Doubts" answers another way, we can see that the students rarely doubted religion because of "bad things religion did in the past" (no. 3) or "getting to know people from other religions, or people with no religion" (no. 7) or "religious teachings about sex" (no. 9). What led to the biggest doubts, then? "The way religious people sometimes pressured others to believe what they believe" (no. 5), "The intolerance some religious people showed toward other religions" (no. 11), and "The intolerance some religious people showed toward certain other people (e.g., homosexuals)" (no. 15).

But again, to put this in perspective, none of these latter doubts averaged even 3.0 ("Moderate") on the scale. Overall,

16

few questions had arisen in these students' minds, and even fewer doubts had developed.[4] Why?

The Paths to Reassurance and the Paths to Doubt

Think back on your own past. What did you do when *questions* arose about religion? Some questions probably came up. "Is there a God?" "Is there really a heaven?" "Why do tornados sometimes destroy churches and miss saloons?" Whom did you go to with these questions? Parents? Priests? Peers?

You might naturally have gone to the people who had taught you the beliefs in the first place. You might also have prayed to God for help, and read scripture or some other book of religious guidance a minister might have recommended. Maybe you talked things over with friends sharing the same religious background.

You do not have to be a psychological genius to know that all of these reactions would probably have *confirmed* the original religious beliefs. The people who taught you your faith, or who share it with you, are not likely to answer your questions with "Hey, I never thought of that. Our religion must be wrong!" If you want to take a wider, more "two-sided" approach to the questions, you would have to search farther afield.

To see what our student-respondents had done, we gave them twelve possibilities, and asked them to tell us (again on a 0–6 basis) how much they had done each of these when

17

questions about religion had arisen. Half of the possibilities would probably have confirmed the original belief:

- Talked with my parents. (2.03)
- Read the Bible or other religious material. (1.66)
- Talked with friends who belonged to my religion. (1.90)
- Prayed for enlightenment and guidance. (1.86)
- Talked with a religious authority, such as a minister, priest, or rabbi. (0.94)
- Purposely went on "retreats" or to "church camps" to renew my faith. (0.88)

The other possibilities involved a wider search for answers:

- Sought out people from other religions, to see if what they believed made sense. (1.24)
- Very critically analyzed each belief. (1.72)
- Decided to believe only what could be proved true, even if it meant giving up my religion. (1.17)
- Purposely read books, plays, and essays that went against my religious beliefs. (0.56)
- Talked with friends who had no religious beliefs, about why they did not believe. (1.71)
- Made a determined effort to get as much information against religion as for it. (0.65)

Not surprisingly, the emphasis placed upon religion in the student's past helped determine how far the individual walked down these different paths. Those who came from strong religious backgrounds tended to take the "seek confirmation" path. Those with weak religious histories tended to explore the "seek wider" path more. How strong were these predilections? Rather weak in the case of the religiously weak, who sought confirmation almost as much as they traveled wider paths, and rather strong in the case of the religiously strong, who sought confirmation much more than they tried "the other side of the street."[5]

Given the drift of their search, you will not be amazed to learn that students with little religious training frequently ended up apostates, or at least religiously "inactive." On the other hand, those with strong religious roots almost always found reassuring answers to their questions, and hence remained active believers.[6]

So all the pieces fit together. In a nutshell, religious emphasis during childhood "pays off" because when questions come up later, the individual turns largely to reassuring sources. Doubts do not develop to any great extent, and the person remains among the faithful.[7]

We do not propose that staying religious hinges solely on the challenge of faith. Some students simply cannot rise to the challenge of getting out of bed on Sunday mornings. Others do, but complain the services bore them. Others rebel against their parents in general, and religion gets swept along as an "innocent bystander."[8] But beliefs can be pivotal for some.

THE IMPORTANCE OF RELIGION TO THESE STUDENTS

If all this makes sense, let's consider the data in absolute, not relative, terms. If you look at the average response to each of the twelve possible "reactions" above, you cannot help but notice how small they are. Students seldom did *any* of the things mentioned. It does not appear that questions about religion, when they arose, stirred them much. Add in the fact that the vast majority of these students seldom go to church, and you sense that religion plays a pretty small role in their lives. Questions about religion probably did not come up very often because these students, overall, did not care very much about the subject. Doubts may be low, but commitment appears to be even lower.

Whatever your views about specific religious beliefs, do you not find this disturbing? After all, religion deals with most of the central issues in life, the "Biggies," and yet few of these young adults have apparently thought much about them. Maybe they will wrestle with them later, in courses and bull sessions. But at this point, most of them appear to have "surfed" over the deep, profound matters that give life meaning, according to philosophers and theologians at least.

That is why we were drawn to the subjects of this book, the "Amazing Apostates" and the "Amazing Believers." For they *have* faced up to the Biggies, to such an extent that they have taken their lives into their own hands. True, they reached opposite conclusions. But they would agree that the matter of religion is far too important to be shrugged off, and that the decision they made in this regard was the turning point in their changed lives. In the next chapter we will begin to see how this happened. But first, who are the "Amazing Apostates" and "Amazing Believers"?

AMAZING APOSTATES

Apostates are defined as persons who have abandoned a religion they once believed in. You will find a fair sprinkling of them in most university classrooms. In our introductory psychology samples, about one in seven students had been raised in some religion, but presently belonged to "none," not even generic Christianity. If you also count students who say they still "belong" to the home religion, but reject almost all that religion's teachings, then about one in four can be called apostates.

As we explained earlier, most of these apostates had pretty *non*religious upbringings, and so their subsequent loss of belief does not come as a surprise. But a few—a very few—came from relatively intensive religious backgrounds, and that *is* amazing. So we rounded up as many "Amazing Apostates" as we could and talked with them. The following chapter tells their story in their own words. In the chapter after that, we shall analyze what they said.

The Definition of an "Amazing Apostate"

Our search for "Amazing Apostates" began with a booklet of surveys answered by large numbers of introductory psychology students at two Canadian universities, the University of Manitoba and Wilfrid Laurier University, in the autumns of 1994 and 1995. The booklet included the sixteen-item Religious Emphasis scale. Here is the scale. Why don't you answer it, on the usual 0–6 basis, to get a feel for what it measures.

Religious Emphasis Scale[9]

To what extent did you have a "religious upbringing"? That is, to what extent, adding it all up, did the important people in your life—such as your parents, teachers, and church officials (if any)—do the following as you were growing up?

> 0 = To no extent at all
> 1 = To a slight extent
> 2 = To a mild extent
> 3 = To a moderate extent
> 4 = To an appreciable extent
> 5 = To a considerable extent
> 6 = To a great extent

1. Emphasize going to church; attending religious services?

2. Teach you to obey the commandments of a supreme, supernatural being?

3. Review the teachings of the religion at home?

4. Teach you to obey the instructions and rules of persons in your religion (such as ministers, priests, bishops, rabbis, boards of deacons) who acted as God's representatives?

5. Get you to read scriptures or other religious material?

6. Teach you to fear the wrath of God and eternal punishment for sinning?

7. Have you pray before bedtime?

8. Teach you that persons who tried to change the meaning of scripture and religious laws were evil and doing the devil's work?

9. Discuss moral "dos" and "don'ts" in religious terms?

10. Teach you to obey government authority ("rendering unto Caesar") so long as it did not conflict with religious principles?

11. Observe religious holidays; celebrate events like Christmas in a religious way?

12. Draw up stricter rules about what you could and could not do than other kids you knew had to obey?

13. Teach you that your religion's rules about morality were absolutely right, not to be questioned?

14. Stress being a good representative of your faith, who acted in a way a devout member of your religion would be expected to act?

15. Teach you that your religion was the truest religion, closest to God?

16. Stress that it was your responsibility to fight Satan and all his disciples all your life?

If your average score was a 3 (a "moderate" amount of emphasis), that would give you a total score of 48. But 48 would be a relatively high score among our students, who averaged 28.4 (not even a "mild" degree of religious emphasis). We noted earlier that these students usually did not have a very religious upbringing.

Once we had identified the students who had a *relatively* religious upbringing, we had to find those who had nevertheless dropped their faith. Since nearly all our students had been raised Christians, we made this "second cut" by looking at their responses to a Christian Orthodoxy Scale. (For those few raised as Hindus, Jews, Muslims, and so on, we also studied other parts of the booklet for signs of apostasy.)

Here is the Christian Orthodoxy Scale. We again invite you to answer it yourself, so that you may best understand how we did this study. Only this time, instead of answering each item from 0–6, use -4 to +4.

Christian Orthodoxy Scale

-4 means you *very strongly disagree* with the statement.

-3 means you *strongly disagree* with the statement.

-2 means you *moderately disagree* with the statement.

-1 means you *slightly disagree* with the statement.

0 means you are completely neutral, neither disagreeing nor agreeing.

+1 means you *slightly agree* with the statement.

+2 means you *moderately agree* with the statement.

+3 means you *strongly agree* with the statement.

+4 means you *very strongly agree* with the statement.

1. God exists as Father, Son, and Holy Spirit.

2. Humans are *not* special creatures made in the image of God; we are simply a recent development in the process of animal evolution.*

3. Jesus Christ was the divine Son of God.

24

4. The Bible is the word of God given to guide humanity to grace and salvation.

5. Those who feel that God answers prayers are just deceiving themselves.*

6. It is ridiculous to believe that Jesus Christ could be both human and divine.*

7. Jesus was born of a virgin.

8. The Bible may be an important book of moral teachings, but it was no more inspired by God than were many other books in the history of humanity.*

9. The concept of God is an old superstition that is no longer needed to explain things in the modern era.*

10. Christ will return to earth someday.

11. Most of the religions in the world have miracle stories in their traditions, but there is no reason to believe any of them is true, including those found in the Bible.*

12. God hears all our prayers.

13. Jesus may have been a great ethical teacher, as other people have been in history, but he was not the divine son of God.*

14. God made man of dust in God's own image and breathed life into him.

15. Through the life, death, and resurrection of Jesus, God provided a way for the forgiveness of humanity's sins.

16. Despite what many people believe, there is no such thing as a God who is aware of our actions.*

17. Jesus was crucified, died, and was buried, but on the third day he arose from the dead.

18. In all likelihood there is no such thing as a God-given immortal soul in us that lives on after death.*

19. If there ever was such a person as Jesus of Nazareth, he is dead now and will never walk the earth again.*

20. Jesus miraculously changed real water into real wine.

21. There is a God who is concerned with everyone's actions.

22. Jesus' death on the cross, if it actually occurred, did nothing in and of itself to save humanity.*

23. There is really no reason to hold to the idea that Jesus was born of a virgin. Jesus' life showed better than anything else that he was exceptional, so why rely on old myths that don't make any sense?*

24. The Resurrection proves beyond a doubt that Jesus was the Christ or Messiah of God.

You noticed, we are sure, the two different kinds of statements on the scale. Half of them are worded in a religious way, and the other half (marked here with an asterisk) reject religious belief. On the average, our students "slightly agreed" with the religious statements, and "slightly *disagreed* with the rejections. So most students endorsed Christian teachings.[10] But the bottom quarter of the distribution did not. Instead, it landed on the negative side of the neutral point, indicating a rejection of the basic tenets of Christianity.

We selected, as potential Amazing Apostates (AAs), all students who scored in the top quartile on the Religious Em-

phasis scale, and yet scored in the bottom quartile on the Christian Orthodoxy scale.[11]

Such persons proved quite rare. In 1994, eighteen were filtered out of 1,457 students who answered the screening booklet at the University of Manitoba. Fifteen turned up among 813 Wilfrid Laurier University students. In 1995, the figures were just 11/1,070 in Manitoba and 14/924 at Wilfrid Laurier. That works out to 1.4 percent of the sample being potential Amazing Apostates. We had to screen over 4,000 students to locate 58 of these rare beings.

Recruiting the Amazing Apostates for an Interview

A few weeks after the students had answered our questionnaires, we sent letters to the potential AAs in each psychology class, asking them to serve in a one-hour interview about their religious beliefs. Reminding them of the recent in-class surveys, the letter explained that they seemed to have traveled an interesting road, from a strong religious childhood to religious disbelief. Would they be willing to tell us about this journey? We promised them a sympathetic, understanding hearing, as well as an "experimental credit" (worth about 1 percent of their grade in the course).[12]

The Interview

We were able to interview forty-six AAs. We began the meetings, which were conducted in our offices, by guaranteeing the student anonymity and obtaining permission to make an audiotape of the conversation. Then we gathered a few background facts such as age and birth order. (The AA Interview Schedule is given in Appendix A.) We verified that, at some time in the past, the student had been much more religious than s/he was at present.

Next, we tried to identify "the tip of the wedge," the first question about religion that had eventually led to apostasy. When had this question arisen, and had the student felt guilty or afraid for questioning the faith? Whom did s/he turn to for answers, and what had happened? Did the parents know questioning had begun? If so, what was their reaction? Who else knew?

We then tried to chart the next steps, the further questions that led to doubts and disengagement. Did the student still feel a member of the home religion? At what age, then, did s/he "break away"? Who knew? Did the student now feel guilt or fear about this decision? How likely was it s/he would go back to the old beliefs someday?

We then began probing hard to answer the question, "Why YOU?"—beginning with a "Back to the Future" fantasy.[13] We asked the students to imagine traveling back in time, to the last age when they were devout. Getting out of the Delorean, they meet their younger self and reveal that someday they will no longer believe in their religion. How would they explain this dramatic change to their younger selves? How would the "younger them" react to this news?

We next asked if the student had experienced other problems with the parents during the time when religious beliefs were being abandoned. Was this a difficult time in general? What had the student's grades been like in school?

Getting right to the point, we explained that while almost

all people question their religion at some point, very few
reject it. "What's different about you, compared (say) with
your brother/sister" or others?

We then posed three questions about the rewards and
punishments of the students' apostasy. What had it cost
them? What had they gained? Then we inquired, "Why not
go back to the 'bosom of Abraham' [i.e., embrace once again
their old belief]? Things would be so much simpler—your
parents/family would be pleased; the world would be simpler;
you would have the security of beliefs and a supportive
church, and so on. Why not go back?"

Next we asked the AAs to imagine that a younger member
of their home religion came to them for advice. Religion had
played a big role in this person's life, but now questions were
arising. This person wanted advice on what to do. What would
they say? (In the 1995 study, we also asked the apostates how
they would rear their children, when it came to religion.)

Finally, we thanked the students for being interviewed,
and asked if we had missed anything important in their stories, or if they wanted to add anything. We also answered any
questions they had about the study.

Amazing Believers

We searched out potential "ABs"[14] among our 4,000+ students by looking for the exact opposites of our Amazing Apostates. That is, we identified every student *who scored in the
bottom quarter of the Religious Emphasis scores, and yet
scored in the top quarter on the Christian Orthodoxy scale.*[15]
Given the overall scores in our samples, this meant we were
hunting for students with almost no background in religion,
and yet very strong beliefs in Christianity. Potential ABs

turned out to be even rarer than AAs, being only 0.8 percent of our 4,264 respondents.[16]

We asked the 24 ABs who gave us interviews almost exactly the same questions we asked the AAs, but with most questions pointing in the opposite direction. For example, instead of pursuing the "first doubt" that had arisen about religion, we asked when the ABs first began to wonder if religious teachings might be true. You can find the complete interview schedule in Appendix B.

In the next chapter we tell the stories of our Amazing Apostates as told to us in their own words. Chapter 3 then focuses on a detailed analysis of the AA cases. Likewise, chapter 4 recounts the stories of the Amazing Believers and chapter 5 summarizes and considers their responses. Finally, in chapter 6 we step back and reflect on what our stories and analyses tell us about these two important groups of students.

NOTES

1. The study is based upon a booklet of surveys answered by 1,070 Manitoba and 924 Wilfrid Laurier introductory psychology students in the fall of 1995. Among other thing, the booklet asked how much the student believed the central teachings of Christianity, how much the home religion had been emphasized while growing up, how often questions about religion had arisen in the past, how the student had tried to answer the questions, to what extent the student now had active doubts about religion, the student's home and present religion, and how often s/he attended church.

Within Protestantism, 96 percent of the Lutherans had been

raised Lutherans, 97 percent of the members of the United Church had grown up in that faith. (The United Church of Canada was formed in 1925 by the union of the Congregationalist, Methodist, and most Presbyterian churches.) Ninety percent of the Anglicans had been brought up Anglicans, 85 percent of the Mennonites had come from that background, and 78 percent of the "Fundamentalists" (Baptists, Pentecostals, Brethren, Salvation Army, etc.) had been raised as such.

(A low percentage should please members of a religion. It means they are winning some converts.)

Similar strong tendencies among people to maintain affiliation with the religion in which they were raised have been noted in other studies (e.g., Hadaway, 1980; Kluegel, 1980).

2. Emphasis upon the home religion was assessed by asking the students how much (on a 0–6 scale) their parents and others had emphasized sixteen different religious teachings or behaviors. The complete Religious Emphasis scale is described later in this chapter.

Summed scores across these sixteen items averaged 28.4, indicating religion was only "mildly" emphasized overall. Correlations among the items had a mean of .56, yielding a "Cronbach's alpha"* reliability of .95, and suggesting that these items constituted quite a good scale, in terms of its psychometric properties.

The importance of emphasizing religion during childhood is discussed in greater detail in chapter 7.

3. Altemeyer (1988), p. 214. In numerical terms, today's parents emphasized religion to their offspring about 70 percent as much as it was emphasized to them when they were growing up. That is, religious training dropped about 30 percent when it became their turn to "pass it on."

---

*Cronbach's alpha is a statistical measure which reflects the "internal consistency" of a scale (as well as the length of the test), or the extent to which the various items are related to each other, and therefore to some uniting theme (such as religious emphasis in the scale above).

31

Sociologists have used the term "drift" to refer to the tendency for apostates simply to drift farther away from the normal religion of their relatively nonreligious home background (e.g., Bahr & Albrecht, 1989).

4. Other studies, for example by Hunsberger, McKenzie, Pratt and Pancer (1993), have also found a paucity of religious doubts among university students, especially among more orthodox and fundamentalist young people. The most doubts, of course, were likely to be found among people who said they did not generally believe basic Christian teachings, and also those who were not fundamentalist in their religious orientation. But even for the "most doubting" students (i.e., those who scored in the bottom third of the Christian Orthodoxy scale), reported doubts averaged only about 4 on the 10-point scale used. The most orthodox students, on the other hand, had even weaker doubting levels, averaging less than 2 on the same measure.

5. To be specific, the bottom quarter of the Religious Emphasis distribution had means of 3.74 over the six Seek Confirmation items, and 5.67 over the six Seek Wider items. The corresponding figures for the top quarter of that distribution equalled 15.30 and 8.37.

You will note that the first set of numbers is far smaller than the second. It makes sense to us that persons with weak religious backgrounds would do less searching of any kind for answers to questions about religion. It has, after all, played a very small role in their lives. But the preference of those who came from strong religious backgrounds for confirmation, rather than a wider search, was pronounced. Over the whole sample, Religious Emphasis scores correlated .65 with Seek Confirmation responses, and only .16 with Seek Wider.

6. This finding meshes neatly with previous work by Hunsberger, Alisat, Pancer and Pratt (1996). They studied high religious fundamentalists (who tend to come from homes which strongly emphasize the family religion) and nonfundamentalists (who are much more likely to come from homes where there was less religious

emphasis). Their investigation led to the conclusion that "high fundamentalists were more likely to report that they had resolved their religious doubts (typically in ways which strengthened their religion) than were low fundamentalists (who tended to report that their doubt resolution had undermined their religious beliefs)" (p. 218).

7. The correlation between Religious Emphasis and scores on the Doubts Scale equalled -.11. In turn, Religious Emphasis correlated .54 with "believing" responses to the Christian Orthodoxy Scale (Fullerton & Hunsberger, 1982), which we shall encounter later in this chapter.

8. For a consideration of the importance of factors such as communication and relationships with parents, see Wilson & Sherkat (1994).

9. We have since improved the Religious Emphasis Scale, which now contains the following items (still answered on the same 0–6 basis):

1. Emphasize attending religious services as acts of personal devotion?
2. Review the teachings of the religion at home?
3. Make religion the center, the most important part of your life?
4. Emphasize that you should read scriptures or other religious material?
5. Discuss moral "dos" and "don'ts" in religious terms.
6. Make it clear that about the worst thing you could do in life would be to abandon your religion?
7. Stress being a good representative of your faith, who acted the way a devout member of your religion was expected to act?
8. Teach you that your religion's rules about morality were absolutely right, not to be questioned?
9. Tell you how wonderful it would be to be in heaven for all eternity?

10. Teach you that your religion was the truest religion, closest to God?

11. Stress that it was your responsibility to fight Satan all your life?

12. Impress upon you that unrepentant sinners would burn in hell for all eternity?

13. Make religion relevant to almost all aspects of your life?

14. Tell you how wrong it was to sin against a loving God?

15. Have you pray before bedtime?

16. Teach you that persons who tried to change the meaning of scripture and religious laws were evil and doing the devil's work?

17. Teach you to *strictly* obey the commandments of almighty God?

18. Get you to do many "extra" religious acts so that the family religion "filled your life?"

19. Make a personal commitment to God as your only hope and savior?

20. Teach you to obey the persons who acted as God's representatives, such as priests, ministers, pastors, or deacons?

In a study of over two hundred parents of University of Manitoba introductory psychology students carried out in the fall of 1996, these twenty items had a mean inter-item correlation of .64 producing an alpha reliability for the scale of .97. In contrast, the 16-item version given in the text had a mean inter-item correlation of .56 and an alpha of .95.

10. Using a 1–9 conversion for the responses to the pro-religious items, and a 9–1 conversion for the answers to the anti-religious statement, summed scores on the Christian Orthodoxy Scale could range from 24 to 216, with 120 being "neutral." The average among our students equalled 147.5. In turn the 24 items had an

average intercorrelation of .66, reflecting the strength to which Christian beliefs are taught as a system in our society. The scale therefore had an alpha reliability of .98. Few psychological measures have such reliability. See Fullerton & Hunsberger (1982) for further information on the Christian Orthodoxy scale.

11. The cutoff points varied a little from site to site, and year to year. A few persons who qualified as "Amazing Apostates" in one instance would not have made the cut had they been in one of the other samples. But only a few.

Additionally, a person could score in the bottom quartile of the Christian Orthodox scale by rejecting many parts of Christianity, but still accepting the existence of God and the divinity of Jesus. To make sure the apostates were "apostates deep down," we checked their answers to verify that they did *not* believe in God or Jesus' divinity.

12. We also included a brief "Pre-Interview Survey" with the invitation, which we asked the student to answer and bring to the interview. It went:

> Some people think that when a person drops most of his/her religious beliefs it is because s/he is becoming critical of many things, not just religion; that this doubting of religion results from a bigger critical attitude toward authorities and social customs in general: parents' beliefs about *many* things are questioned, school teachers are viewed with less respect, social customs about being "good" and "obedient" are downplayed. According to this theory, the general moving away from authority and customs begins first, in many ways, and the dropping of religious beliefs comes *later*, as *one* of the results. Other people think that the change in religious beliefs is most important and comes first. The person is not "rebelling" in general, but instead first has problems believing in the family religion. Then, after the person has decided to no longer believe what their

family and church want them to believe, they may (or may not) start breaking away in other ways. But the religious beliefs went *first*, for their own reasons, not as part of a general criticism of what authorities have taught. Which theory best describes what happened to you?

We never did reach eight of the 58 potential AAs we had worked so hard to find (five in Manitoba and three in Ontario). Our letters simply remained uncollected in the classrooms, despite repeated attempts. Of the remaining 50 whom we did reach, four declined to be interviewed (two at each site). Everyone else made an appointment and kept it.

13. This exercise was based on the popular *Back to the Future* series of movies. In fact, when we asked if our participants had seen one of these movies, *all* of them had, and all had little difficulty grasping the idea of traveling back in time in a "Delorean," where they could meet their younger self.

14. "Apostasy" is a term with an extensive history in the psychology of religion literature. Our use of the phrase "Amazing Apostate" in this book is therefore intended to conjure up in the reader's mind an exceptional kind of apostate—one who abandoned her religion against considerable odds. But at the "other end of the spectrum," there is no readily available terminology to describe people who become very religious, against considerable odds. We initially thought of calling these people "Amazing Converts," but abandoned the phrase when it became clear that some of them were *not* converts in the traditional sense of the word at all. They had not joined any established religion, for example, but they *had* become much more religious than they were earlier in their lives. So we settled on the term "Amazing Believer" (AB) to describe this sort of person.

They certainly are "believers," though the actual content of their religious beliefs differs considerably from one person to the next, and their behavior does not always match their beliefs. They are indeed "amazing" because they became highly religious in their own way, in spite of having grown up in homes where there was little if any religious influence.

15. We looked for all people whose Religious Emphasis scale scores were below 12 (the bottom quarter of the distribution on the scale, which can range from 0 to 96). We then looked for people from this group who indicated, on the Christian Orthodoxy scale, that they substantially accepted basic Christian teachings. That is, they scored above 188, or in the top quartile of Christian Orthodoxy scores.

16. In the two Manitoba studies, eleven potential ABs were identified in 1994 and nine in 1995. At Wilfrid Laurier, five and nine were spotted, for a total of just 34 out of 4,264 respondents. We could not contact three of these students despite repeated efforts, all in Manitoba. Three of those we reached in Manitoba, and four of those in Ontario, declined to participate. So we ended up interviewing 24 of the 34 potential ABs (or 71 percent, compared with the 79 percent of the potential AAs we interviewed).

2

Interviews with the Amazing Apostates

We shall begin by presenting, in some detail, sixteen "case histories" from the forty-six we collected. We selected most of these cases because they are typical; that is, most of them reveal themes we heard often in these interviews, as well as their own unique features. We have also included a few "off-quadrant" cases to show the less-traveled routes to amazing apostasy. We shall give brief summaries of the remaining thirty cases at the end of the chapter. The next chapter will present overall summary data on the entire sample of forty-six interviewees.

To protect these students' identity, we shall not describe them by school, community, and so on. We have changed the gender of about half of our participants, and made other minor alterations in order to protect their identity. We have also given them pseudonyms in alphabetical order, alternating female and male.

ANNE

Twenty years old, Anne was born the fifth child in a family living in a predominantly Catholic town outside a large city. Like her older brothers and sisters, she was given a "strict Catholic upbringing" by her mother. Her father did not go to church, and neither of her brothers does now. On the other hand, her two sisters remain quite religious.

In her responses to the Religious Emphasis scale, Anne indicated that going to church was strongly emphasized in her childhood, as were obeying the Ten Commandments, praying before bedtime, and observing holidays such as Christmas and Easter in a religious way. It was stressed that she should always be seen as a good representative of her faith. Believing in Catholicism as the truest religion was also emphasized, as was fighting Satan.[1] But her answers to the Christian Orthodoxy scale indicated Anne now rejects virtually all the traditional teachings of Christianity. She believes in a "God" that created the universe, but not a personal God.

Anne says she was very devout all the way through high school, until age seventeen, when she started seeing things differently. "I just started making up my own mind, and stopped believing basically about church, and what they were saying was right and wrong."[2] The pope became the "tip of the wedge" for her. "The pope can't be flawless if he's human."

Where did Anne take this first question? Interestingly, she did *not* go to her parents. "It would just have made my mom angry." Nor did she consult with a priest. Instead, she discussed religion with two friends at school who were also questioning things. Before long, Anne began to resent "having to act so proper and obedient in church" and the way the church was "always asking for money." And she began to see different meanings in the Bible: "No matter what you look at, you can interpret it in different ways. They just want you to believe in one. It becomes sort of 'Reflex' competing with 'Thinking.'"

Anne broke off going to church when she was eighteen. At first, she had to work on Sunday mornings, which her mother accepted for a while. But that "cover" eventually became transparent, and by now her parents know Anne does not want to go to Mass, especially if she has been out late on Saturday night. Her mother's only response has been an occasional, "Maybe you can go to church today." But no "scenes" have erupted (possibly because of earlier battles with her older brothers). Her parents have never asked Anne about her new views on religion. She does not feel fearful, or guilty about them. "Everyone has a right to decide. There are so many religions in the world. Catholics are right and all the others are wrong?"

At this point the interviewer challenged her. "Suppose someone were to say to you, 'You stopped going to church because you're lazy. You just want to go out and drink on Saturday night, and that means you don't go to church on Sunday.'" Anne responded that if God is everywhere, why do you have to go to church? And she did not believe you had to be a Christian to have good morals, that in fact Christians often hurt others, and are hypocrites. By way of contrast, she had noticed (when she was twelve) that one of the happiest and nicest families in her town never went to church. Anne thought it "very unlikely" she would ever go back to her old beliefs. They held no attraction any more.

Asked how the sixteen-year-old Anne (the last age at

which she was devout) would react in the "Back to the Future" scenario, she replied that her younger self simply would not believe she could lose her faith, especially in such a short time. Encouraged then to explain to her former self what had caused such a big change, Anne said, "You start hearing different people's ideas: movies, just friends talking, books." What books? "Any books. Like *The Hobbit*. Everything can be in a different realm. All those things make you think that there are infinite possibilities."

Anne says she did not have problems with her parents while in high school. "They were not strict on curfews." They approved of her friends. She had been a "very good" student in school, especially in high school.

On the pre-interview survey, Anne said her loss of religion arose from a general critical outlook that developed first. She remembered criticizing the educational system, doubting that a lot of education was really going to prove worthwhile. She also concluded at an early age that politicians are liars.

Pressed to explain further why she had "gone against" her strong religious upbringing, Anne said, "I didn't like being told how you should interpret different readings. Why can't you make up your own mind?" She was also turned off by inconsistencies in church teachings: "They say we're all equal, but they also say that Christians, especially Catholics, are better than others." She felt with all the racism and sexism in the world, people should try to eliminate barriers between themselves, and accept each other.

In terms of losses and gains, Anne regrets the way some of her aunts look down on her now. She also misses various old friends who avoid her. What makes these losses worthwhile? She now decides things for herself. "I don't believe what people tell me to."

41

What is her main reason for not going "back to the bosom of Abraham"? She balks at the notion: "You have to believe what you're told. There are people dying because of over-population, but the pope is against birth control. And saving your soul is the most important thing. But we don't know if there is a soul."

Placed in the hypothetical situation of advising a younger, strong Catholic who is questioning her religion, Anne said "I definitely would not tell her to drop her beliefs. I'd probably say something like, 'You have a mind, you can think, you can figure stuff out. If you're not sure, talk to other people.' I would not want to influence her."

BILL

Bill, age twenty-one, has a complicated family background. His parents divorced when he was just three, and he is one of five children from his original family. He has two other siblings from his father's remarriage, as well as two whom his stepmother brought to that marriage. However, Bill grew up mostly with his mother and original four siblings, visiting his father on weekends.

Bill believes his parents' divorce stemmed partially from their religious differences. His father belongs to a fundamentalist church and became "extremely religious" after the divorce. Bill was very involved in his mother's Anglican church, and his father instilled a strong fundamentalist orientation as well. Accordingly, Bill answered almost every item on the Religious Emphasis scale with a 5 or 6, producing one of the highest total scores in the sample. He became serious enough about religion at one point to consider becoming a minister.

What took him from this path? It began with a little thing. He matter-of-factly told a friend, when he was about eleven, that since the friend was not "born again," he was going to burn in hell. The friend disputed this, arguing it was more important to be good. He also got Bill to thinking about whether eternal hellfire could exist, which his father had made him very afraid of.

As Bill got older, "I really got into mythology. If we don't believe any more that there is a guy that carried the world on his shoulders, why should I believe that I'm going to burn in eternal hellfires if I do this." Bill indicated on the pre-interview survey that such religious questioning preceded any "general critical outlook."

Bill discussed his emerging questions with his mother, and received some comfort and assurance from her. "My mother always said it is completely natural to question, and I would go through a stage where I would definitely question . . . and that was my choice. [But] my father never was really that open about it."

Bill's questioning continued into high school, "and a lot of that was because of the type of friends I got into." He was put into a gifted program and found that some of the other gifted students read about Satanism, briefly perking his own interest in the subject. Meeting a lot of people from other cultures and other religions also led him to wonder why any specific religion was better than another. Eventually he began to suspect that religion might just be "a huge cult. I view my father and his entire family as completely brainwashed and practically like they are in a cult."

43

Bill is now reluctant to say he belongs to any particular faith. "When I was younger I would have said I was Anglican just because that's the church I grew up in. Now, I haven't figured it out yet. I would say I'm still searching." He has chosen some university courses to help sort out his thoughts on religion. "I think I did a lot of research and am still conducting research into religion."

Although Bill feels "completely justified in questioning," he still carries some guilt over his apostasy, mostly "because my father still doesn't know. He still thinks that I am a perfect Christian." He acts and dresses "totally differently when I'm with my father. I know he would just feel horrible if he knew the truth." Bill is considering marrying a non-Christian, and "I know that my father will really flip out when he finds this out."

Bill thinks it very unlikely that he will ever return to religion. "Those things aren't nearly as important to me as freedom of thought and freedom of expression. My father certainly is important to me, but if it means me having to conform to something that I simply don't believe in, I can't do that."

When confronted by the "Back to the Future" scenario, Bill thought that his five- or six-year-old self would have been quite shocked at the changes. But by the time he was nine or ten he would have had some realization "that I was coming towards that type of thing." He would explain that it was in his peer groups that he "started learning and talking and studying, and I realized that maybe I didn't want to be a Christian after all." Bill would tell his nine-year-old self, "You are too young to realize how much influence and control that your father has had over you. When you begin to learn more and talk to people, you will realize how limited and focused that certain area of religion is. There is a lot more out there."

Bill has real problems with *faith* per se. "When I ask people who are very religious what keeps them believing, and all those people say is that they have faith, I can't understand for the life of me what this faith is. How can you believe in something that is completely intangible? A lot of these people just haven't looked into other forms of religion, or learned about mythology as I have. They have questioned, but they didn't research other religions."

The reader should not assume that Bill dislikes his father, in spite of disagreeing strongly with his religion. "My father means a very great deal to me. I know that some day I am going to have to tell him that I don't have these beliefs and it is getting closer. Now that I am living with my girlfriend, I can't keep that from him forever. Loss of respect from my father is what I'm beginning to fear most."

Bill feels he has gained from his apostasy though, especially in terms of "social and educational freedom. I am a lot stronger than I would be if I had let Christ control my life instead of making my decisions. I am a stronger person. I think that I have had a much wider social range than if I was living with my father's view of religion, in which case I would only associate with Christian people."

If a nine-year-old came to him with questions about religion, "I wouldn't say give up religion. I would just say don't believe everything you're told. Although you might think that parents are always right, they are not always right." He would encourage the boy to do some reading and thinking about religious teachings.

CLAIRE

Claire, age twenty at the time of the interview, grew up on a farm in a prosperous Mennonite community. Both her parents believe strongly in the "traditional" Mennonite faith, and they raised their four children to be just as religious. Claire has an older sister, and two younger brothers.

According to her answers to the Religious Emphasis scale, religion had been greatly stressed throughout Claire's youth. Besides going to church and praying a lot, she was taught over and over to obey God's Commandments. It was also emphasized that she should follow the guidance of church authorities. Her parents and others told her that the Mennonite faith was God's true religion, and its rules about morality were absolutely right, not to be questioned. Those who tried to change the meaning of scripture, she learned, were evil and doing the devil's work. She was taught to fight Satan every day of her life.

Remarkably, most of this emphasis became sort of the clothes she wore every day, but not the person inside them. Talking about her early adolescence, Claire said, "I considered myself religious then, but when I look back I wasn't." Aside from family activities, "I didn't live out my faith. I didn't pray, I didn't even know where my Bible was."

When asked why all her parents' efforts had so little effect upon her, privately, Claire answered, "I don't know. I've asked myself that so many times. I think it's because I question. . . . I don't believe things about the Bible just because my parents tell me. I want to see it."

Claire began to question Christianity at age thirteen,

46

wanting to know "Why?" and "How?" She could not remember the first question, but she volunteered the most frequent one. "Why can't anyone prove that (e.g., Christianity, the Bible, that Jesus actually lived)? Why should I believe it?" Claire reports she now "always questions everything," but (as she indicated on the pre-interview survey) her religious doubts arose first.

Her parents did not know any of this was happening within their teenage daughter. She hardly realized it herself until she was seventeen, at which time she was attending a Mennonite boarding school. Then "I'll never forget the day it happened to me. . . . It hit me I wasn't even a Christian. It took me a long time to come to terms with that . . . I didn't like the insight." Claire thought it was "bad" not be a Christian, and it took her "one or two years" to stop feeling guilty over abandoning her religion. But "I couldn't make myself believe it."

Claire did not reveal this dramatic change to her family. But eventually they noticed, around the supper table, that her views on smoking, dancing, alcohol, and women's rights differed from everyone else's in the family. Big arguments would break out, Claire vs. Everyone Else.

Her parents still do not know how completely Claire has rejected Christianity. Her mother says things like "Claire, you say you don't believe in the Bible, but really you do." Her parents expect her to "come out of this phase" later in her life. However, Claire thinks it very unlikely she will ever believe in Christianity again.

In the "Back to the Future" fantasy, Claire said the sixteen-year-old version of herself would react to news of her apostasy as follows: "I wouldn't be that surprised that it had happened, but I would be surprised at the peace the twenty-year-old me had found." Why? "I realize I am not a bad person, even though I am not a Christian. To the sixteen-year-old me, that would have been unheard of." Why did Claire change, then? "I didn't have any choice. I can't make myself believe something that I don't believe." But the sixteen-year-old Claire "didn't have enough knowledge" to understand this.

Claire described her parents as being "very, very passive." While not accepting her behavior, they never yelled at her. They did not make a big deal out of the difficulties she occasionally got into during adolescence. She said she got very high grades in school without having to work.

Asked to explain why she abandoned her faith when almost everyone around her has remained Mennonite, Claire focused on the behavior of her Christian friends. "They'd say they're Christians because they say they believe in God, and they go to church usually. And I say, 'That doesn't make you a Christian. What makes you a Christian is believing all that, and living it out.' They don't live it out." They do "far worse things than I do," and that makes them hypocrites.

The interviewer then asked "How come they can be hypocrites, and you can't?" Claire replied "the difference is . . . I have to be true to myself, I have to be honest."

Dropping her faith has cost Claire acceptance within her family. Besides her parents, her older sister is quite devout and does not understand. Her younger brothers adopt the family view that Claire is "the 'black sheep' in the family, completely, totally."

What then makes this worthwhile? "I know who I am, not what my parents want me to be. I'm still very confused about a lot of the things I believe in, but at least I'm becoming who I am." Why is Claire so different from her sister, then, who is quite content to be what her parents wanted her to be? "I don't think I can help it. It was not a choice I made. I didn't *want* to stop being a Christian." She could not go back because "I do not believe it. I could not make myself believe it. I would not be true to myself. I'd be lying to myself."

The situation of giving advice to a budding apostate turned out *not* to be hypothetical in Claire's case. Several people had approached her in such a context. "I don't want to push what I believe onto them, because they'd start believing what I believe. I said, 'You have to find out for yourself what you believe in. That doesn't mean ignoring what your parents tell you. You have to decide if that is what you want, if that is what you believe in.' "

DWIGHT

Twenty-one-year-old Dwight is the youngest of three siblings. His Catholic family went to church every week when he was growing up, and Dwight attended Catholic elementary and high schools, and was involved in youth groups, church plays, and choir. All in all, it was a strong religious upbringing, reinforced by a close-knit ethnic community. Dwight describes his parents as "pretty hard-core Catholics."

At age fifteen he began to have serious questions about Catholic teachings concerning homosexuality and premarital sex, and "creation also became an issue." His girlfriend at the time helped to initiate some questioning, but it was a difficult process. "I felt guilty for the longest time. I mean, I don't know if you stop feeling guilty. It seems like you are turning away from something that you are supposed to believe and everybody else believes in."

49

Dwight and some school friends discussed religious issues: "one person would take the side of evolution and someone would try to defend the religious side." Many of his friends had grown up in "almost an exact same background" and many remained believing Catholics, so the discussions were quite lively. However, Dwight pointed out that "it is nice to know that there are other people out there having these thoughts and it is not just because you are a bad Catholic and you are turning away because you are rebelling against something."

Dwight expressed concern that the Catholic church presents just one side of issues, and as a youngster he didn't even realize there *were* alternative perspectives on issues such as creation. "You don't have a choice. They only give you one side and that's what you have to believe in." He contrasts this with the university, where "you've got a chance to learn the other side."

Dwight's parents had no idea that their son was questioning religion, though he did share his concerns with his sisters, who have continued to be practicing Catholics. When Dwight came to the university more than two years before being interviewed, he found it even more of a challenge to the religious beliefs he had been taught when growing up. In particular, he did not find other Catholics on campus to bolster his Catholicism. Instead he was matched with a roommate who was a "big evolutionist."

Dwight still identifies himself as a Catholic, attends church irregularly, and does accept some Catholic teachings. "I don't think you can just turn away. No matter how much you try to turn away from them, you still believe them. If something drastic happens in your life, like a death, you will turn back and pray."

Dwight's parents still do not know about his doubts, especially since he still attends church when he comes home from school, but his peers do know about his real beliefs. He still occasionally feels guilty about his turn away from religion, "especially around holidays, times that my family spends doing a lot a religious things together."

There is very little chance that Dwight will return to what he believed as a child, "just because I don't believe in it." But he does intend to raise his own children as Catholics, "and then give them the chance to decide later on in life if they don't want to be Catholic."

When we played "Back to the Future," Dwight said his younger self would be quite shocked, and "would think I was an evil person." He would explain to the surprised youngster that "you're only taught one side of the story. They can't prove half of what you are believing in and the Bible is not even written by the people you thought it was written by. When you learn a different side, then you have enough knowledge and you can make a choice."

Although he had some conflicts with his parents in discussions of things like premarital sexuality, Dwight feels that these were just "relatively normal teen-parent interactions" and they have never had any major conflicts.

How does he explain his disengagement from religion when his sisters have remained quite active Catholics? "I don't know if they have had as many influences on their lives from people who are not Catholic, and who have a lot of questions about Catholicism. That pushed me away from it." When the interviewer pressed the issue of *why* Dwight doubted religious teachings more than others do, he concluded that his friends and acquaintances had stimulated more questioning in him. "We were not taught to question. You didn't question, you believed. But when someone comes up and says, why do you believe this, you can't answer why you believe it. After a while you don't have any answers any more, and you start to question yourself. Well, why do I believe in it?"

There have been costs in Dwight's rejection of religious teachings. "When you do believe in God you always have somewhere to turn. It is almost a comforting feeling. You would lose that." On the other hand, he has gained freedom of choice. "It's my choice now. I decided what I wanted to believe in, not what I was forced to believe. I've seen both sides of the issue."

Why not return to the "bosom of Abraham?" "You can't go back. I would have to change my lifestyle and that is a little too much to ask." In addition to knowing homosexuals who are *not* "bad people," Dwight said that premarital sex and contraception have become part of his life, and "I'm not going to stop."

If a teenage boy came to him for advice concerning questions about Catholic teachings, Dwight would "suggest a few good books. I would give him the other side of the story or places to go where he could find the other side of the story. I'm not going to tell him this is wrong and this is right. But you can tell him to listen to the other side, maybe sit in on a few university lectures." Ultimately, if the advice-seeker "has the information in front of him, he can make a choice. He can decide Catholicism is the way to go, or he can go the other way."

Finally, Dwight observed that "I really liked growing up in the Catholic faith. I don't know if that sounds strange because I don't believe in it now, but as a child, it was good. I would raise my children in the Catholic faith because I think it was excellent growing up with it. They give you a lot of excellent values, things that children should grow up with."

ELEANOR

Eleanor, twenty-three, is an "only child" in a Lutheran family which attended church only on special occasions such as Christmas and Easter. However, she took intensive confirmation classes for several years, and was actively involved with a church youth group. By the time she reached her mid-teens, she was attending church regularly on her own. Although she has always gotten along "pretty well" with her parents, Eleanor believes that she "had a lot of problems as a kid." She was diagnosed with a hyperactivity disorder, and got into fights with other kids. But after grade six she went to a new school, and then "I turned my life around." Her grades were quite variable, ranging from "not so good" (though always above average) to being best or second-best student in her classes. Although she "hardly ever studied," she read extracurricular books with considerable interest.

Eleanor began to have questions about religious teachings when she was about fourteen. She feels that her interest in science might have contributed to her questions about biblical teachings. She says she never did believe the creation story, but "I didn't discount the possibility that God could have created us through evolution." The biblical story was therefore "just symbolic. But the reason I really started questioning was they were trying to tell us that Lutheranism is the only religion . . . and they'd always put down Catholics and other Protestant denominations. I found that closed-minded and not in accordance with the teachings of the Bible." She also decided that the Bible was written "to conform to the political structure at that time," and this limited its applicability today to, for example, the question of women's rights.

Eleanor's questions caused some anxiety, since "you are taught that you have to go this way or you'll go to hell." Near the end of her confirmation classes she gave a speech "intended to really question a lot of the beliefs." However, "it was so subtle I guess that nobody really caught on to it and they were all saying it was such a great speech." This made Eleanor feel guilty, since she appeared to be supporting religion when she had meant to question it.

She did have some discussions with her minister about her questions, but found the answers to be unsatisfying. Sessions with a devoted Christian friend were much more influential. The two friends would often debate Christian teachings, with Eleanor taking the questioning position, and her friend defending religious beliefs. Similar discussions occurred in a high school English class. Eleanor's purpose in these debates was to make religion work for her. "I was trying at that point to tie everything in to a religious framework that would allow me to believe in Christianity." But she couldn't find the answers she was looking for, and became less religious. She also hunted for answers in the Bible, which she read every evening before she went to bed. Eleanor misses those readings even today, "because it gives you a focus and if you believe in it, you have all the answers you're looking for right there in the Bible." But they were answers she could not accept.

She did have some discussions with her parents, but "never conveyed the extent of my questions." Mostly, it was her friends who really understood the breadth and depth of her questions, and who really know where she stands on religion today.

Eleanor now considers herself an agnostic, having stopped thinking of herself as a Lutheran in a religious sense when she was about seventeen. However, "I'm still a member of the Lutheran church. I still go on Christmas Eve and all that," and "if I get married, I'm going to get married in a Lutheran church." She is now at peace with her agnosticism and no longer feels any guilt or fear because of her beliefs. "Just because I don't believe that Jesus Christ was the son of God, I'm not going to be damned to some eternal hell, if there is such a thing. It just does not make any sense to me."

If she could find some way to reconcile religious teachings with her current belief, Eleanor could conceivably go back to being an active Lutheran. But it isn't likely because "I just don't believe that, really, any religion has the absolute answer."

In response to the "Back to the Future" scenario, Eleanor said that she would tell her younger self about the intolerance, contradictions, closed-mindedness, and so on that she saw in religion. Her fourteen-year-old self would have been surprised at all of this, and "a bit stubborn," but she "would have gone home and thought about it and then started looking at things on her own."

Why is Eleanor different from most people her age, who question but then accept religious teachings? "I have always considered myself to be really analytical of things. I can't knowingly have two beliefs that contradict each other." Also, it would be hypocritical to pretend to believe in something that she cannot accept, something she believes many "religious" people do.

Eleanor says she really wanted to believe in religious teachings, and tried hard to do so. Since becoming an agnostic she has "tried to search for other things to guide me in life." But she still hasn't found anything which answers

55

"deep philosophical questions" like "what's the point of existing and what happens after death?" She recalls that "the Bible provided a whole framework for actions. It really gave you a lot of reassurance. That's why a lot of people believe it—because they need something to reassure them." She even mused that "if I get older and start thinking about death, maybe that will drive me back to the Bible because I'll want something to believe in."

Eleanor feels she has gained a lot from her apostasy. "I find I can be a lot more open-minded about things, and judge them for myself rather than always trying to tie them into the religious context." Also, "science makes a lot more sense" without having to interpret it in religious terms.

She has talked with her friends about the possibility of returning to her religion, but concludes that "I just can't make myself believe something that goes against my personality." However, if she has children, she would "expose them to the Bible and have them attend confirmation classes and all that, and let them form their own opinions. I'd try not to be too biased. I'd just like to let them come up with their own opinions."

If a fifteen-year-old, beginning to doubt her religion, came to Eleanor for advice, she would "try to talk to her within a religious framework as opposed to my framework," and "ask her what she has doubts about, and express my views on the matter. But I'm not going to tell her religion is bad and you shouldn't be a Christian. I would try to be sensitive, to have her think about it, and ask her why she believes certain things and have her explain that." In the end, it would have to be the fifteen-year-old's own decision whether to believe in religion or not.

Reflecting on her life, Eleanor emphasized that her apostasy was not rebellion against authority. Rather, "it was . . .

a clear-minded analysis I made." She is quite comfortable in her current agnostic position, and enjoys discussing religion with her friends.

FRANK

Eighteen-year-old Frank is the oldest of four children born to a couple living in a mid-sized city. His mother attended Anglican services regularly. But his father, while agreeing with the teachings of the Anglican Church, did not like "the way the church was run," and so he stayed home on Sundays. So did the children as a rule. But dinner conversations often revolved around Christian principles, and the day's news was interpreted in religious terms. The Anglican faith was presented as the truest religion, and scripture reading was stressed. Yet "it wasn't a 'doctrine' religious upbringing, but more of a way of thinking."

Frank says "I never really questioned my religion for a long time. I guess I first really heavily thought about it when I was fourteen, in grade 9. Before that, I really didn't think about it. It was sort of like, my family said this, and I had no reason to think about whether they would say something that wasn't true."

In grade 9 Frank was hospitalized for quite a while with a serious illness. "For a long while during that I felt that God would come and save me somehow. But after a while I started thinking that this wasn't going to happen, and I was just going to have to find some way out myself. And once that happened, I started questioning lots of things. Eventually, by the end of grade 9, I decided that Anglicanism is definitely not the way to be thinking about this." He thought these religious doubts came before any "general critical outlook."

By age eighteen, Frank accepted almost none of the traditional teachings of Christianity. He does not find an "order" to the world and asks himself, "If God is omnipotent, how can he allow Satan to continue operating, unless he doesn't care?" He also sees a lot of the images and metaphors in the Bible as irrelevant now. "There aren't a lot of sheepherders any more."

Frank stopped considering himself a Christian three or four years ago. "I have a lot of Jewish friends. My family jokes that I'm more Jewish than Christian because they say I've been to more bar mitzvahs than church services. But I wouldn't call myself a Jew either."

At first he felt both guilty about questioning his family religion, and afraid of what would happen if he did. But he did not take his questions to anyone, and instead tried to figure things out for himself. "That's generally how I do things." Eventually Frank realized that questioning things was not something he should be punished for. After that, "I became a little cocky."

By now, four years later, Frank's parents realize that his religious beliefs have undergone a serious change. But they never sat down and talked about them with him. "My parents were not really very strict about anything. If you did something, they just watched you do it. Then afterwards they would point out my mistakes. But if it looked like it was sort of a debatable thing, they stayed away from that." He does not feel guilty or afraid any more about abandoning the family religion. He thinks it "unlikely" he would ever return to Christianity.

Frank is majoring in fine arts, and he revealed that "a lot of my art is directed toward religious themes." Thus for a recent basic design assignment, he turned in a box built such that "when you looked in one end, you saw a Star of David with a cross inside it, and when you looked in the other end, you saw a pentagram."

Asked to be "Marty McFly" and go zipping back into the past at 88 mph in the Delorean, to meet his eleven-year-old self walking home from school, Frank said his younger self would be shocked at the change. For one thing, the eleven-year-old Frank refused to wear denim, and now this "hippie" would come up and say "I'm you in just seven years." He also thought that, if his younger self found out what lay ahead in terms of religious beliefs, he would start doing everything he could to make sure it did *not* happen. Frank thought he would have trouble explaining the transition, and would just blurt out something like "God does not exist!"

Predictably, Frank did not have many problems with his parents, "the way most people did. I generally got along with them well." He got A's "in most subjects" in school. His parents are happy he has chosen to major in fine arts.

He remains the only person in his house to have broken with religion. But in the larger context of his aunts, uncles and cousins, his family comprises the "black sheep" of the clan because they seldom appear in church together.

Frank said his religious change came with a price. "Certainly there's sort of a loss of innocence. I think about things more than I did then, I worry a little bit more. Before I would have thought everything will turn out all right. How could it not? Now that's a question." Asked what he had gained from his new perspective, he immediately replied, laughing, "I've got more to draw about." "But in terms of concrete things, I can't think of anything." Frank read Robert Pirsig's *Zen and the Art of Motorcycle Maintenance* a few years ago, and came away with the idea of "karma" as a good thing, if very indefinable.

Frank thought his parents would want his return to the Anglican faith to be his decision. The interviewer then "made a pitch" for returning, in terms of knowing what to believe, being supported by a community of fellow believers, and having an expectation of eternal happiness if he did the right things. "How can you turn your back on all of this?" Frank said the concept of heaven was pretty unrealistic. "How can you be happy forever without getting bored?" The interviewer replied, "Religion teaches that the presence of God is so magnificent, you would never get bored. Why can't you believe that?" Frank replied, "I don't really have any reason *to* believe that."

What would he say to someone from his own background who was beginning to waver in his faith? "I would probably not give advice as such. I'd probably describe my own situation, and say 'you can believe something similar.' It's not my place to direct. I'm not a traffic light. It would be his choice."

GINA

Gina's parents are from an east Asian country, and she is the middle of three sisters. Her family attended church every week and more often on important occasions, when she was growing up, and religion was clearly important though not excessively so, in her view. This is consistent with her Religious Emphasis score of 48, which was not as high as some participants', but certainly high enough to be included in our sample. Gina attended a Catholic elementary school, and was involved with the church youth group for about a year. Gina was on the honor role throughout high school, having received mostly A's and B's in her elementary and high school years. "I loved both elementary and high school."

It is only within the last year or two that Gina has begun to be less accepting of religious teachings. Her primary concern in this regard has been the Catholic church's teachings about birth control, divorce, and women's issues. In addition, Gina is a biology major, where she has come to accept the evolutionary explanation of human origins. "The scientific approach sounded more logical." She thinks she was just more accepting of things when she was younger, "because I didn't look into things, I just accepted what was said."

Gina initially experienced some guilt about her questioning because her parents did not (and still don't) know about it, and they would be upset because they are "fairly religious." However, she no longer experiences these guilt feelings. The only people she has talked with about her questions are her friends (both those who are religious and those who are not). This has helped her sort out some of her questions. In spite of her strong disagreement with some church teachings, Gina still considers herself to be a member of the Catholic church, and her Christian Orthodoxy score of 112 indicates that she still at least weakly accepts some church teachings.

Is she likely to return to a more accepting view of the church? "I don't think so, because . . . it's the whole women's status things that still get me. So, unless their views change about issues like that, then I don't think mine will either."

Gina did not hesitate in responding to the "Back to the

Future" scenario. "I've become a little bit more educated, a little bit more aware, because I wasn't aware beforehand about a lot of the views that the Catholic church held. So it's just a matter of me learning what those views were and deciding whether or not I felt the same way and obviously I don't." Her younger self would be very surprised at this change. However, she feels that the seventeen-year-old Gina would also accept this explanation since, "If I had gotten that information when I was fifteen, sixteen, seventeen, I probably would feel the exact same way I feel right now. So I think it was just a matter of when I got that information."

Gina had "regular problems" with her parents, mostly about how late she could stay out. "They would yell, you would scream back, and it would be over." But she never argued with them about religion, and does not feel their disagreements about issues like "curfew" were serious.

Why is she less accepting than many of her peers? "I won't accept what I've been taught if it doesn't feel right to me. Just because my parents or a teacher or a priest or nun says something . . . if they believe it, that's fine, that's their prerogative. But if it doesn't feel right to me then I can't accept it." She added that she does not feel she is an overly critical person "at all. But it's just certain things, if they don't feel right then I won't accept or believe." Why not simply go back to the church and accept its teachings completely? "It still wouldn't feel right."

The only cost of her loss of some beliefs is the possible upset to her parents, if they learn her real views. So far, Gina has continued to go to church with them when she is home, and this has avoided any confrontation. On the other hand, she feels she has gained faith in herself, in what she believes in, and is more confident in her beliefs.

Whether or not Gina raises her children as religious will depend on her husband. "They would definitely be baptized. I would probably send them to a public school, or I might even send them to a Catholic school for the first couple of years, so that they can get an idea, like I did." The baptism would be primarily to please the grandparents. She mentioned that she would probably take them to some different churches (e.g., Catholic, Anglican). But in the end, they should make their decision on their own.

What advice would Gina have for a seventeen-year-old who was beginning to question her religion? Gina would recommend that she think about "what she believes in and what aspects feel right to her." In addition, she might suggest talking with friends. She could not recommend a teacher or priest "who would try and sway you back, probably." But Gina herself would not try to guide her to an answer. "It has to come within herself."

Asked if there was anything she would like to add, at the end of the interview, Gina said no, "I think the basis of my decision was whether or not it felt right. That's the main thing. That is why I changed some of my views, because they just didn't feel right."

HARRY

Harry, age nineteen, was born the third of four children raised in a very devout Jehovah's Witness family in a good-sized city. He stands out in our survey data for having an extremely high religious emphasis score. He answered all but three of the sixteen items with either a 5 or 6. Religion basically filled Harry's free time during his childhood, as he attended church five times a week, read the Bible and Witnesses' publications at home, and prayed with his parents.

His father in particular reviewed the faith's teachings and discussed morality to a great extent. The instructions of church authorities became "law," and persons who questioned these were condemned. The Jehovah's Witnesses were considered God's true religion. Satan was everywhere, trying to change the meaning of scripture, and Harry was taught to fight the devil all his life. He attended Theocratic Ministry School, where young Witnesses are taught how to proselytize door-to-door. He then went on such expeditions. In short, Harry was raised to be a model Jehovah's Witnesses youth.

Imagine then the interviewer's astonishment when Harry revealed that he never believed "any of it." He felt religion had been "hammered" into him, and he greatly resented not being given a choice about his beliefs. "Right from the beginning, when they made me do something, I didn't like it. I did give it a chance. But I guess it was just spite that made me not want to do it."

Harry said that he was not a rebellious child. He would obey his father and mother in all ways when he was young. "I always tried to please my parents. But they were trying to control every single aspect of my life. And after I turned sixteen, I decided that was enough. Religion took about 75 percent of my time, and I just didn't want to do it any more."

The first question about religion that arose in Harry's mind, well before he was twelve, was "if God really does exist." Next he wondered, "Is the Bible the word of God? Or is it something just made up to keep people in line?" Then he began to wrestle with the "problem of evil." Asked why his religion's answers to these questions did not reassure him, Harry said, "They just weren't satisfying enough. Most of it was contradictory. For example, if God is perfect, then everything he created would be perfect. But it isn't." His religious doubts arose before any general critical outlook.

The pivotal event in Harry's life came at sixteen, when his parents arranged to have a church official come into their home for an hour each week to see "if I would go farther" in the Jehovah's Witnesses. This person asked him what he believed. (Harry said it was the first time anyone had asked him, rather than told him.) Harry uncloaked his secret, whereupon this "advisor" told him to stop the charade with his parents.

Harry thought it over for two weeks, and then did so. After six hours of intense debate, during which his mother and father brought up the arguments that Harry had heard all his life, and he revealed the counterarguments that had been swirling around in his head for years, his parents realized their son did not believe in their religion. (His three siblings quickly revealed that they, too, did not believe, and none of the children in the family attended church thereafter.)

The Witnesses community sends members to the house almost weekly to try to win them back. And Harry's father will occasionally read passages from *Watchtower* aloud, and ask for Harry's reaction, which he gets, and then "retreats for a while." But Harry feels he still is not his "real self" around his parents. "My parents don't know I drink. They've never known that I've had a girlfriend in my entire life, which I've had behind their back. They have no idea I have a sex life. I got very good at hiding things."

Harry did not think he would ever become a Jehovah's Witness again. "I've had so much, that I pretty much know all that they have to say. There's nothing they could say to make me come back. Even the magazines they put out. I've noticed they've been putting out the same stuff again and again."

Harry said he had no problems with his parents when he was a teenager. He was the "especially good" child, as far as they knew. He got A's in school. They did not know his friends because Harry did not invite them to the house. "I never really brought them around the house much, because the few times that I did, my dad would get into preaching to them, and they wouldn't appreciate it."

Asked what was so different about him, that led him to turn his back on such a strongly emphasized religion, Harry said he knew other young Witnesses who did not really believe. But they were too afraid to reveal this. When he was twelve, he had seen several people "disfellowshiped," and no one in the congregation was allowed to talk to them again. Even after these people repented and asked to rejoin, they were not accepted. The message seemed clear.

Pressed again to explain how, knowing the price he would pay, such an "obedient kid" could defy the family's religion, Harry repeated that he always resented not being given a choice: "I was sent along this path that I didn't like very much." He also resented missing holiday joys (including Christmas), and having to stand outside his classroom each day while his classmates sang the national anthem.*

Harry was not at all tempted to "go back to the bosom of Abraham." In fact he said the Jehovah's Witnesses' vision of heaven ("eternal servitude to God") was not all that attractive. Asked to imagine advising a young questioner, Harry

---

*Jehovah's Witnesses regard many holidays as pagan, and pledge allegiance only to the Kingdom of Jesus.

said, "I'd probably tell him to write down all his questions, and then delve way deep into the Bible. See if he could find answers. If he could find them, then good for him. But if he couldn't, I would then say 'Stop doing what you're doing. Break away from it.'"

When asked at the end of the interview for any other relevant factors that had not been discussed, Harry said, "Well, my dad has a temper. He would go off for the littlest thing, and we would get beaten. This went on until I broke off [age sixteen], and as soon as I broke off, that was the end of that."

IDA

Ida, nineteen, and her younger brother were born into a Roman Catholic family. However, soon after the parents were married, Ida's father joined a fundamentalist church, and so Ida grew up in the middle of this "split religion" family. Her mother took her to mass every week, and she attended a Catholic elementary school. "Looking back on it I think it was almost a competition between them to see which side I would end up on." Add to this church summer camps, missing school to observe religious holidays, active participation in youth groups, and you have a young person who had an incredibly high level of religious teaching and involvement. From Ida's perspective, it became "just ridiculous."

Her marks were "horrible" in her early grades 1 to 4, "usually C's." Then she changed schools and the grades improved to mostly A's and B's by high school. "I never really worked that hard and I always got pretty decent marks." Ida did have some social problems at elementary school, which she attributes to the severe restrictions placed on her weekend activities by her father's religion, which made her feel quite "alone."

When she was fourteen, her father forced Ida and her brother to quit sports (in spite of her mother's objections), because they had to practice on Saturday ("the sabbath"). There was no television on weekends, and they were not allowed to go to dances or many other social functions. "I was always kind of ashamed of going to church with my dad because I couldn't go to the school dances and people would wonder why aren't you going out on Friday nights. By the time high school came it was just ridiculous. I would never tell people. I would just lie—for figure skating I just said I didn't like it any more."

The parental religious differences contributed to marital tension. Ida's mother objected to the amount of money her father gave to his church, for example. Also, her father insisted that the family spend each summer vacation at an expensive seven-day church function. "Finally, my mom kind of got fed up with that because she would go there, then my dad, my brother, and I would end up going to church half the time."

Ida remembers, "I went to church with both of them until I was about fifteen, and that's when I just kind of got fed up with it and I just told them I wasn't going to church any more." More surprising, when asked if there was a time in her life when she was much more religious than she is now, she responded that, although she *knew* a lot more about religion because of the intensive teaching she received, "I don't think I ever really fully believed what I was being taught . . . I think I've always had doubts."

Ida's earliest doubts involved the different religions of her parents. "I saw two different groups of people who had very strong beliefs and who were just worlds away in where they were looking. And I've always had doubts for that reason." By age eleven, feeling considerable pressure from both parents' religions, Ida had decided that "I wasn't going to commit to either church" and she refused to go through confirmation in the Catholic church. It wasn't until years later, when she was about seventeen, that she started to question specific teachings and doctrine such as the existence of God, and decided that she did *not* belong to *any* religion.

She felt guilty doubting because her father made it clear that when problems or doubts occurred, it was Satan's doing. Ida didn't talk with any adults about her doubts because, "I've always felt that ministers are going to have a very one-sided view of their religion, obviously. I had a subscription to the [church publication] and there was a youth magazine. . . . I had kept my subscription just because I never really felt like canceling it. I would always browse through it even up until I was about seventeen. I've always kept an open mind."

Ida and her brother discussed their concerns about religion, and she had a few brief conversations with an uncle, but that was about it. The uncle had many problems in his life, and Ida blamed this on her father's religion. "I saw what happened to him and associated that with what would happen to me if I stayed in the church." Ida is sure her parents never did appreciate her religious doubts and feelings. "Once I left my dad's church, I don't think he really cared any more. I guess he just kind of gave up on me." Both parents now probably "know at this point what I think," though her father "usually just says I'm crazy. He doesn't take it really seriously to heart, and doesn't want to talk about it."

Ida feels no guilt or fear at all about her religious views now, and it isn't very likely that she would every go back. "Something divine would have to happen. I can't sit there and listen to something that I don't agree with. There's just too much doubt."

In the "Back to the Future" scenario she said that the thirteen-year-old Ida would *not* be surprised at the changes that had taken place. "I think that I realized that I needed to get away from that church but I was afraid. It was a gut feeling that I should leave but there was still that pressure to follow the bigger path, the clearer, the easier way, at that point." If we went back farther, say to the time when she was eight, she *would* have been surprised, because the eight-year-old Ida "was just more accepting of everything."

How would she explain the changes? "I have more confidence now. Before, I always tried to fit in because I always felt in a sense that I didn't, just because of my religion. Now, I'm going to go and if you want to follow me you can come along. I'm not as concerned about getting in with people, whereas before I was just a follower."

Ida did not have serious problems with her parents other than the substantial conflict over religion. She tried pretty hard to keep her private life to herself. For example, after she had left the church, when she went out on Friday nights (which her father would disapprove of), she simply slipped out without making an issue of it.

Ida feels she is different from her still religious peers because of her unique experiences. "I see more of an overview of different religions. I can see through the propaganda whereas other people might not be able to. I obviously had to question it because I couldn't live two religions my whole life. I was forced to decide which one was wrong, and I just came up with the conclusion that neither one of them was wrong or right." Ida does not feel she has lost much in her struggle to free herself from religion in her life, though she said that "middle age would probably be an easier time to decide something like that." On the other hand, she had no problem pinpointing the main benefit of no religion in her life—*freedom.*

She has thought about how she will raise her own children, but still hasn't resolved the issue. She would "definitely celebrate Christmas and the traditional holidays, but I don't think I would go to church." However, "if their father wanted to go to church, I would never get in the way." If a ten-year-old came to her for advice about religious questioning, "I don't think I would press my ideas on her, but I think that I would just say 'go with your feelings, with your heart.' I would be acting as one of the ministers if I went and pressed my ideas on her."

Ida has come to believe that religion is full of hypocrisy and at least some religion "rips people off." "You don't want to see somebody get conned out of money or something and I almost feel that's what is happening to my father." In addition, "most people believe there can only be one true religion, and there's a lot of them [religions] out there. I mean the odds are that yours is not going to be it, then."

JACK

At eighteen, Jack is the oldest of four children raised in the Baptist faith in a large city. He attended church twice each

Sunday while growing up, and was involved in church youth activities. His parents strongly emphasized obeying God's commandments, and those of church authorities. Prayers were regularly said in the home. His parents explained moral "dos" and "don'ts" in religious terms, and Jack felt he had to obey stricter rules of conduct than most children did. Satan was everywhere, he was told, tempting him. The Baptist faith, he heard over and over, was God's true religion.

When he was young, Jack believed deeply in his religion. But at age eleven or twelve, he began "to get critical about things." He could not recall the first teaching he questioned: "I just started questioning a lot of the stories, like how Adam and Eve could have populated the earth. There would have been a lot of incest. It just seemed to be a myth. And also about the existence of God. I trusted that if I prayed, I'd get what I asked for, and I didn't."

While Jack did not feel guilty about questioning his religion, his parents became upset when he brought them his doubts. A "continuous discussion" developed, as more questions evolved. His parents did not seem to have answers, offering instead "It's just faith" or "It's just because." His parents understandably became upset at Jack's "drifting away," especially when the next sibling in line followed in his wake. "They think I'm a negative influence on the children."

Jack summarized his current position as follows. "I've pretty much come to the conclusion that I don't believe in it. I don't have faith in Christianity. But there still are questions. Sometimes I still wonder. I don't have the absolute answer that God doesn't exist. But I also don't have very much need to believe that he does." He had reached this conclusion, and "left" the Baptist religion, in his mind, by the time he was fifteen or sixteen.

Jack told his parents then that he no longer wanted to go to church. They insisted however, that as long as he lived at home, he had to attend services every Sunday with the rest of the family. Jack then got a job which gave him an excuse for skipping this weekly excursion. But on those Sundays when he does not have to work, he still goes to church. "Sometimes I listen, sometimes I daydream. My parents are hoping that one day I'll come to the realization that the Christian faith has the right answers for me. That as long as I'm going, there's always the chance." He in turn has "told them a million times" that forcing him to go is only creating resentment. "But they do not seem to want to accept that."

Sometimes, Jack says, "I question whether I've made the right decision or not. If they're right, then the Bible says I'm going to hell." But he nevertheless thinks it very unlikely he would ever go back to being a Christian.

If the eighteen-year-old Jack climbed out of a time-travelling Delorean and told his younger self that his religious beliefs would eventually disappear, he thought his younger self would be shocked. How would he explain this great change, then, to "young Jack"? "I'd say it [religion] doesn't make life any different. It doesn't give help in the way he would have expected."

Did Jack have other problems with his parents during adolescence? Yes. "We were not getting along well. There was a lot of arguing over things. I wanted to do things, ordinary things, and we fought over curfews." His father had lost his job, and that created a lot of turmoil. Then a grandparent died. "It was all just a really big shock to us, just mass confusion." But in school Jack always got good grades. "They'd always push me harder than the other kids. I was always at the top of my class."

At this point the interviewer, too, pushed Jack harder, asking the "Why you?" question. Jack had said, on the pre-interview survey, that a general critical outlook had preceded his religious doubts. Asked to explain, he said, "I always asked questions about why we do things. It was curiosity. My parents did not punish questioning. I'm not really afraid of authority. I accepted it, but did not fear it." Jack added that he noticed early that authorities had their failings. "I viewed my parents as hypocritical. They try to believe. But they don't always show what they're believing, what they're supposedly following. That's always been a big issue for me. I've heard them say one thing, and then do another."

In terms of costs, Jack believes his parents have lost respect for him, and they think that he quit Christianity to spite them. They also feel "they went wrong somewhere along the way," causing Jack to lose his religion. "They can't understand why I couldn't simply have faith." Jack considers this to be the biggest gain from his decision. "I don't trust blind faith. It's just wrong, and it can lead you into a lot of trouble. Also, I've had my eyes opened to a lot of things, such as the narrow-mindedness of Baptists condemning homosexuality."

Jack firmly rejected the idea of returning to the bosom of Abraham. "It doesn't fulfill my needs. I understand all that. I've heard it all my life. . . ." What needs would it fail to fulfill? "It's almost like a searching feeling. That there's something out there that I haven't figured out yet. And since I've grown older, and become more of an individual, separate from my parents, my religion never seemed to accommodate that searching feeling."

Jack's advice to a young Baptist beginning to question his faith would be "to ask himself if this is what he wants to believe in. He should find out more information, and ask

someone who is knowledgeable. It would be better for him to
ask a minister than to ask me. I don't want to be responsible
for someone losing his faith."

As regards raising his children in religion, Jack said he
"would not force them into religion as much as my parents
did. But I probably wouldn't have to do much, because my
mom would want to take them to church. It doesn't seem fair
to not allow them to experience that."

KATHY

Kathy, age eighteen, was the second-born child to a devout
Catholic couple living in a "bedroom suburb" of a medium-
sized city. According to her responses to the Religious Emphasis scale, she had about the most religiously intense background of all the Amazing Apostates we interviewed. Part of
this emphasis came from attending Catholic schools up
through junior high. But mostly it resulted from Kathy's parents' strong devotion to the Catholic faith. Kathy went to
Mass daily and became an "altar girl." She prayed throughout the day, was taught to treat priests and nuns with rever-
ence; feared Satan's temptations and God's eternal punishment; had to live within strict rules of religious conduct; was
expected to be a model Catholic; and believed Catholicism
was the one true religion, most favored by God.

Kathy said she was a "good Catholic" until age twelve. "I
was not a rebel." But at that time the family began attending
a church in the city, where only boys were allowed to perform
altar service. When she asked the parish priest why, he al-

legedly responded, "The only thing girls are supposed to do in church is sing." She asked why, and the priest's response was basically "The pope says . . ." As her old priest had criticized the pope at times, an argument ensued. She left it feeling the Church was set up mainly to benefit men.

Kathy took her question of "Why are women so unequal in the church?" to her religion class in school, and was rebuffed. This led her to ask more basic questions: "Is there really a heaven and hell?" and "Is there really a God?" The teacher's response was "Don't ask that," and eventually Kathy was thrown out of the class. Kathy lost respect for the teacher, deciding he did not know enough to give sensible answers to sensible questions. This soon generalized to other teachers, whom Kathy noticed "taught out of the teacher's guide. It turned out they often had only a grade 12 education." The school phoned her parents, who told her to "shut up" in class. When she did not, her mother and father began calling her, angrily, "the devil-child."

Kathy said that while she was hurt by her parents' reaction, she did not really expect them to see her side. In her mind, they seldom had, showing instead a preference for her older brother. "Whenever something would go wrong, I'd be blamed right away." Eventually, however, Kathy's brother developed a serious drug problem. "I told my parents," she said. "It would have been easy [to stop him], but they went to see this nun, and they did nothing about it. Just prayed."

Kathy did not want to be confirmed at age twelve, but was forced to go through with the ceremony. "I look so angry in my confirmation picture!" By the time she was fourteen, she no longer thought of herself as being a Catholic, or anything. She told her parents that if they sent her to a Catholic high school, "I would just get myself expelled," so she got to attend

76

public school. There, a world history teacher taught about conditions in Third World countries, "where so many children are dying of starvation, but the pope only wants more children so there can be more Catholics."

Kathy no longer lives at home, and seldom speaks with her parents. She never felt guilty or afraid for "asking questions, which is what got me into trouble." She thinks it very unlikely she would ever go back to Christianity.

If time traveling enabled her younger self to see the future, the eleven-year-old Kathy would not be surprised. "I knew then that this whole religion thing, they get you when you're young. Why not wait until you're older, and if you want to be baptized, then let people ask?"

Kathy had big problems with her parents during adolescence, which centered on the favoritism shown her brother. "He is so spoiled. My parents would buy him $80 shirts, and if he didn't get them, he'd cry for them until he did. They totally worshiped my brother." She gave a different picture of herself: "I was grown up enough to know when I had to get my homework done. They never had to tell me what to do. And I was always the one to clean up around the house, and my brother did nothing." She was not, however, a good student in school. It took a lot of hard work to get B's in grade 12.

Kathy acknowledged that she dropped her religion partly because of anger at her family. "I just totally went against my parents. I resented the fact that my brother was the fair-haired child, and they called me the 'devil-child.' That made me more against them, and I started getting my own brain." But she still thought that even if she had not had a brother, her days as a Catholic would have been limited, "because I just did not agree with the whole religion. I couldn't follow something I didn't agree with."

Her loss of faith has cost her nothing, Kathy feels. Her relationship with her parents was doomed anyway, she said. As for gains, "I'm myself. I think I'm a stronger person due to not having a religion to fall back on every time something goes wrong. Instead of running to the Church, I'll face the problem." Accordingly, the interviewer's description of the joys of returning to the fold elicited only a smile. "I find religion is for weak people, and I don't find myself a weak person. I don't have to follow someone else's morals. I have my own. You get them from common sense, and thinking."

What advice would Kathy give a potential apostate? "Talk to your priest, ask questions. Read. Educate yourself. You can't just sit there, and accept what they're saying. You have to read, and see if you agree with what they're saying. You have to have your own mind. Maybe she'll agree with me, maybe she won't. It's her choice. If I were to try to make her *not* be a Catholic, that would be just as bad as what the Church does."

As for her own children, Kathy said, "When they get old enough, I'll tell them I was Catholic. If they want to be, then 'Go ahead.' "

LANCE

Lance's mother was a strong religious influence on her three sons. They went to church every Sunday, he sang in the choir in elementary school, played the trumpet for church functions, and sometimes "did a few readings" for school masses. After his parents separated when he was fourteen, Lance lived with his mother. His father was not particularly religious, but had sometimes joined the rest of the family in going to church in the years before the separation. After the divorce his father became more religious because his girlfriend is "another fairly religious person." Lance had a difficult time dealing with his parents' divorce, especially since he was "a sympathetic ear for both sides, which caused a lot of problems for me." He did argue with his mother after his father moved out, but such problems "came and went."

Lance remembers being much more religious when he was younger. He attended Catholic elementary and high schools, although the high school was selected for its better music program, not for religious reasons. He had marks "in the 90s" right through elementary and high school, except for his last year of high school, when they dropped into the 80s, because, he says, he didn't enjoy school as much that year.

Questions about religion appeared when Lance was just seven or eight years old, and got "standard Catholic answers," which he grudgingly accepted. He admits that he didn't put much thought into his questions at this point. The first one he remembered involved proof for religious teachings. "I didn't see any evidence of [God's existence] in the world." Toward the end of elementary school Lance began to question more intensely, and serious doubts arose when he began high school. He was concerned about media reports of priests abusing children, and wondered how people could "be killing in the name of God" as they did during the Crusades.

When Lance was fourteen, he got a job which required working into the wee hours of Sunday morning, at which point he began to sleep in instead of getting up for church. His mother accepted this, grudgingly.

Lance experienced some guilt about questioning his religion because he felt he was disappointing his mother. Initially, he approached both parents with his questions, but found that "the answers were basically the same as Catholic teaching, God exists, all this stuff." Although his father was not as devout, he was careful not to encourage Lance's doubts. However, Lance did detect "sarcastic overtones" to his father's answers, and he stated that "I didn't get the impression from him that he believed himself, entirely, even though he was telling me that he did." Lance found all of this "kind of confusing" and it did not help him to sort things out. He also talked with both religious and nonreligious friends, which helped a bit. But the friends who were religious "just believed, so there wasn't anything that they could say that would convince me."

When Lance stopped going to church, it was his father who agreed he should stay home and sleep in, but his mother was not very happy about it. His mother still "requires I go to church on Christmas and Easter, while I'm living at home," and pushes him to go to church every week. Lance thinks his parents must have some appreciation of his religious attitudes, but not a complete understanding of them. His mother "keeps pushing, not hard enough to push me away, but hard enough just to keep the thought there." His father probably has a better idea of Lance's real religious views, but is willing to leave the decision up to him. Probably only his close friends know exactly what his feelings are about religion now.

Although he personally has not identified with Roman Catholicism since the age of seventeen, Lance pointed out that "I was born Catholic, I can't change that." While it is unlikely that he will ever go back to his earlier religious beliefs, he does not rule out that possibility. He no longer feels any guilt or fear about his religious views.

80

In the "Back to the Future" scenario, Lance would tell his younger self that as he grows up he will develop a more scientific mind, and therefore need more proof before he believes things, "and basically the Catholic religion isn't going to provide that for you." His younger self would not be especially surprised at this. "I think I probably did see it coming for a while, but didn't recognize it."

Lance had trouble pinpointing why he is different. He pointed out that he and a friend are very similar in all sorts of ways, but the friend is a devout Catholic, and Lance cannot explain the difference between the two of them. He just finds it harder to accept religious teachings. He did note that his two younger brothers seem to be "going the same way I did." Lance does not feel he lost anything by becoming less religious, but neither has he gained much. He did mention that he doesn't have to follow strict Catholic teachings anymore, and after a bit of prodding, said that his apostasy "does give me peace of mind . . . it relieves a lot of the doubts that I was having." He sees no reason to go back to the church, "basically the only thing that would really be different about my life would be the fact that I'd be going to church on Sundays." It would also make him feel like a hypocrite because he doesn't believe the teachings.

Would Lance raise his own children "in the church"? That would depend a lot on his wife and her approach. He would be willing to take his children to church "for their sake and for hers." If his wife was not devout, he would probably not take his children, unless they asked him to. In the end, he wants his children "to be free to choose what they believe." Similarly, if he were giving advice to a questioning ten-year-old, he would be careful not to steer him in one direction or another. "He should be free to choose for himself."

Lance currently classifies himself as an agnostic, and says, "I can't see myself changing my views . . . there really is no way for me to get proof of the existence of God, so I will probably always have doubts and I'll never really know exactly what's out there." Interestingly, at the end of the interview, Lance commented that, looking back on things, he *might* have continued to be religious if the Catholic church had not tried to "*force* everything on you."

MAUREEN

Nineteen-year-old Maureen is the middle of three children raised in a conservative Jewish family who went to synagogue and observed the sabbath. Although the family decreased its observance of the sabbath and special days as the children grew older, Maureen was clear that her parents remained quite religious. She also attended Hebrew school for eight years, for about two hours a day, three days a week, outside of regular school, and occasionally participated in other religious activities.

When Maureen was younger she just accepted Jewish teachings, because "I didn't really know any better." However, when she was about eleven, after about six years of attendance, Maureen started thinking, "why am I going to Hebrew school? I don't really believe in what I'm being taught." This was the beginning of her questions, which developed "to the point where I'm not at all religious now."

The first specific questions involved Bible stories. "Adam and Eve—does that make any sense or would evolution make more sense? Is there a God? That kind of thing. Are these stories that I'm being fed really true? I know that I'm Jewish, my blood is Jewish and I'm always going to be Jewish and I'm proud of that. But as for the religious aspect of it, I can't accept what I was taught." She also disliked the sexist nature of her religion. "Why participate in something where I am a second-class citizen?"

Maureen did feel a bit guilty "that I was disappointing my mother, because I remember saying this to her and I remember thinking that would be a disappointment to her that I didn't believe in what she believes in." When Maureen got a bit older, she also talked with her friends about her religious questions, but initially it was just her mother, who turned out to be more understanding than Maureen had anticipated. "I'm lucky because she allows me to think freely and I wasn't repressed or anything. She accepted, and still accepts, that I feel this way, but I assume she still thinks I am going to marry someone Jewish." Maureen gets along well with both parents and continues to be quite open with them about her views. When she and her parents left a recent important service she told them, "this is probably the last time I going to go. I'm agnostic and that's it. They just kind of accepted it. They didn't say, no, you have to go, or anything."

However, Maureen is not sure that her mother's response made any difference in her continuing doubts. "I was going to think the way I was going to think no matter what. I have a mind of my own. I'm going to view things my way because that is how I feel." Her father was aware of her questions, and he, too, showed tolerance. Maureen shared her feelings with some other close family members, but hid them from other, more extended family (e.g., grandparents and an aunt), because she felt they would be much less accepting.

By the time she began high school, Maureen saw herself as Jewish in an ethnic, but not in a religious, sense. If someone asked her if she was Jewish, she would say yes. "But if I had a discussion I would let them know my beliefs, that my background is Judaism, but I don't accept the teachings." Today, she feels no guilt or fear about her apostasy, and is "100 percent" sure that she will not return to Jewish religious beliefs, even if it made her parents happier and her life simpler. "Why should things be simpler? Who said life is easy? It would actually be kind of boring if things were simple. But I don't like the teachings. If I took back the knowledge that I know now and I decided to believe in it anyway, I would just be lying to myself."

The thirteen-year-old Maureen would "probably not be too shocked" if she found out about her future religious beliefs, "because at that point I was beginning to question, but I hadn't actually come out and said it." A couple of years earlier she would have been surprised, and "probably perturbed. I'd probably be kind of angry that I had spent so much time being taught all these ideas that happen to not be true." She would say, "As you get older and you begin to see things for yourself, you start to develop a mind of your own. You start to question things and you start to look around and you don't just take for granted what you are being taught is the truth. You start to question everything. You start to see things in a new light."

When asked to explain why she is different from most people who accept religious teachings, Maureen replied, "I think it is hard to shake brainwashing that has occurred from your childhood on. People that adamantly believe in their religion, often it is their parents' beliefs put on them and they just grew up accepting that. Maybe they just don't bother to question or they really do believe it. It has been ingrained into their minds very strongly. What's different about me? I guess I'm just a skeptic. It's just my personality. I'm a questioner."

Maureen could not think of any costs to her apostasy. Rather, "I've gained because I'm not in the dark. I've opened up my eyes." In addition, she mentioned gains in self-awareness.

If she has children of her own, Maureen will not send them to synagogue or to Hebrew school. But, "I wouldn't force my views on them. If they want to shop around and see which is their own, what they prefer, that's fine. But it would be very hypocritical of me to force one on them."

If a ten-year-old girl came to her for advice concerning her religious questions, Maureen said she "wouldn't discourage the person from believing in religion. For some people, religion is the answer. But if she has questions, I would probably explain my views, and say she has a right to have questions. There are other ways of looking at things. It doesn't have to be one way. If I was close to this person, I might help them explore these other avenues."

Finally, reflecting back on her religious changes, Maureen mentioned that the lack of other Jewish children might have been a factor. "I was raised in a city with a small Jewish population. There was nobody in my elementary school who was Jewish, and there was only a handful at my high school. So maybe the fact that I wasn't raised with Jewish kids has something to do with it."

NICK

At twenty-three, Nick was four or five years older than most introductory psychology students. The only child of a single mother living in a small city, he was raised in the Lutheran faith. He attended church every Sunday in his youth, and religion was emphasized at home. Nick learned to obey the commandments of a supreme being, which were presented as absolutes and not to be questioned. He feared God's punishment, read the Bible a great deal, discussed morality with his mother in religious terms, and observed Christmas and Easter as religious events. He went to Bible camp every summer as a child.

Nick said his mother stopped taking him to church when he was ten, apparently after a romantic relationship she was having ended. Thereafter his early training, his friends, and their parents sustained his beliefs for a while. However, as he entered adolescence, Nick made a new set of older friends with whom he began to smoke cigarettes and drink alcohol. Asked how he squared this at the time with his Lutheran upbringing, he replied "If you pray, you can get forgiven."

At age fourteen Nick and his mother moved to another part of the country, where he again made two different sets of friends: one group was quite religious, the other was getting into drugs. By the time he was fifteen, "I still went to church once in a while, I still believed in God, I still prayed. But it wasn't as important to me. My friends and the fun I was having took priority." But he soon began to question his religious training. "I thought, 'Gee this is so great. We're all having fun, nobody's getting hurt. What's really wrong with it?' "

While Nick did not feel guilty about his new activities—even though he started skipping school and his grades slipped from A's to C's—he did feel great fear that God would punish him for transgressing. "I think that religion used the tactic of fear on me, and I don't think that was right because my idea of God is that he would be forgiving. Yet they would tell you these things like 'You're a sinner and you're going to burn in hell.'" Nick's mother did not know all that was happening with her son. "I kept it hidden. When I later told her everything, she didn't want to hear about it. I guess she thought it was a reflection on her parenting."

When he was sixteen, Nick began exploring other religions, and went to different church services. Finding none that suited him, "I decided I was not a church kind of person." He thought his overall rejection of religion stemmed from a more generally rebellious, critical attitude that had shown itself earlier in his skipping school and sneaking into bars. He also remembered thinking, at an early age, that "politicians were a bunch of money-hungry people who just like to throw their weight around."

By the time he was nineteen, Nick had broken with Christianity completely. "The questions I had were never answered. Why am I here? Who created God? And when I asked people, they either completely avoided the question, or said something really bizarre like 'You have to have faith.' That wasn't enough for me." Nick thinks it is very unlikely he will ever become a Christian again. He feels no guilt about that, and no longer fears punishment as he does not believe in God.

If sent back to the past to reveal the future to his twelve-year-old self, he said the younger Nick would be upset. Why? "Because he thinks that Christians are the good people, and someone who isn't a Christian is obviously evil." How would he explain this change to his earlier self? "I would tell him it was okay, there's nothing to be afraid of. I found the truth. The people that he's listening to are lying to him, and are trying to frighten him into belief."

Despite his misadventures when he was a teenager, Nick did not have "parent-child" trouble with his mother. For one thing, she had "a liberal outlook." For another, she "was preoccupied with her own situation. We were always close. But I did not tell her exactly what was going on in my life."

When the interviewer pushed to the heart of the matter, and asked why he had lost his religious beliefs when most persons from strong religious backgrounds do not, Nick answered, "I'm thinking for myself. And I'm looking for answers in my own way. If I have a question, I ask more than one person. And I don't believe things as quickly as I used to."

When asked, "Well, why is this true of *you*?" Nick replied, "I'm a stronger person than most." The interviewer then suggested that the Lutheran Church would probably not agree, but would say instead that he had been seduced by Satan. "When you should have been in church and school and associating with God-fearing youth, you were cutting classes, sneaking into bars and doing drugs. The church might well say you ended up this way, not because you were strong, but because you were weak." To which Nick replied, with some feeling, "I'd tell them that I am definitely a stronger person. I'm not going to live my life as somebody's puppet. I have a mind of my own, and I can think for myself, and I won't be forced to believe in things that are ridiculous."

Nick did not think he had lost anything by giving up Christianity, but had only gained. "I can't be fooled. I can't be told I'm a bad person. I'm not afraid of death, or life. The biggest thing is, I'm not afraid, I'm not living in fear. It almost makes me sick to think that religion would use fear on children, who are so vulnerable."

When the interviewer painted as attractive a picture as he could of what would happen if Nick went "back to the bosom of Abraham," Nick simply smiled and replied, "It's not true. None of it's true. And I feel sorry for those who believe in that. I think they're underestimating their own strength, and they should give themselves credit for their strength, not some superior being. And I think they're fools."

Nick said he would tell a young questioning Lutheran not to worry. "There's no such thing as hell. Keep asking questions." However, "if this person really felt that bad about questioning, I would say 'Pray for forgiveness.' If I said, 'Don't believe in any of that,' that would be overwhelming at such a young age."

OLIVIA

Olivia, age twenty and a third-year university student, was the youngest of four children raised on a farm; her father believed strongly in the Catholic faith. Her mother, raised in the Greek Orthodox religion, had become a Catholic, too. Olivia attended church every Sunday while growing up, and learned the Commandments and other traditional teachings as unquestionable absolutes. Persons who challenged these were doing Satan's work. She was taught to obey priests and higher church authorities. She helped with altar service for five years, and prayed nightly before going to bed. She felt she had a "strict upbringing," and had to follow a more demanding code of conduct than most of her peers. She was frequently told to be a good representative of the faith.

In all of this, Olivia was following strong family tradition. Her grandparents were all "very, very religious." Her siblings were raised as she was, and reacted the same way. Accordingly, Olivia described her faith as follows. "I basically wouldn't question the word of God. That was the absolute truth. There was none of my own thinking. What my mom and dad thought, that's what I thought."

All of this held together until grade 12, when Olivia attended a five-day university enrichment program in anthropology, which opened her eyes to the history and diversity of humanity. "It's not a two-thousand-year deal I'm living in, but millions of years. It began my questioning of the whole 'Jesus thing.' " When she entered the university at eighteen, "through educating myself in different courses I really began to question certain things. I found things that I had done before seemed ridiculous. I saw that religion was developed to explain the unexplained. And as we are advancing, religion is getting pushed out because we're explaining things that it had explained as something totally false."

Asked which courses had led to this conclusion, Olivia mentioned sociology and human physiology. Her sociology course portrayed religion as something developed to control society. The text pointed out how religion had to keep modifying its teachings "to keep up with technology and new knowledge that would prove them false." In physiology, studying how the brain works had led her to believe "everything's physical."

For a time, Olivia's doubts made her "ridiculously afraid. Sometimes, I would cry myself to sleep just thinking about death, about what it means that when I'm dead, I'm dead.

Religion makes people feel safe about death, thinking there is something afterwards." She had lost that assurance. Olivia discussed her doubts and fears with a few close friends, but never told her parents of the change taking place. "There is no questioning at home. I feel I am in a different time zone than my parents. I have talked a little bit to my mom, asking her if she really believes we are going to live for billions of years (after we die). My mom does not fully understand it either." But Olivia fears her parents will find out what she really believes, so she goes to church when she is at home. She knows she will have to get married in a Catholic church, although she has not considered herself a Catholic since age eighteen. Olivia does not think a generally critical outlook led her to reject her faith; religious doubts appeared first. She thinks it unlikely she would ever believe in Christianity again.

How would the seventeen-year-old Olivia react to news that she would soon lose her religion? "I think I'd definitely be emotionally troubled by it. I'd be definitely distressed. I would probably go to my parents and talk to them, to keep it from happening." Then how would the twenty-year-old explain this tremendous change to her younger self? "I'd say, 'You'll start learning new ways of thinking when you get out of the small town concept. There's a lot of narrow thinking when you're in a small town.'"

Olivia had "no major problems" with her parents during adolescence. "I always wanted to do what I wanted to do, and they would try to constrict me." Arguments occurred over how she spent her money, and how often she could go out with her friends. She got "at least A's" in school. "My mom hounded me every week. I had constant pressure to get good grades."

Olivia answered the "Why you?" question in two ways:

first, she believed many young adults from strong religious backgrounds want to break away, but cannot. "A lot of people are always battling it inside them. Only a few people come out and say it. People who don't believe in God are still scared to even put that down on a survey." Secondly, when asked what enabled her to fight out "this battle," she said, "If you talked to my mom and dad, they'd say that I think about stuff twenty-four hours a day. I constantly think about and analyze things that I could never absolutely answer."

Olivia's loss of faith, in her opinion, has cost her a fair amount. "Sometimes when I go to bed, when I have only myself there, because I am so close to my parents, I realize that when they die I'm never going to have them again. It was better before. Ignorance is bliss. Maybe that's why religion was developed, so there wasn't this huge hole." But Olivia had a simple answer to what she had gained: "knowledge."

The interviewer then played the role of a parish priest trying to win her back to Catholicism. Olivia responded "It is not a personal choice thing. If I had the choice, I would do that. But once you think something, it's not gone, it stays with you. You can't just get rid of it. I can't believe it." She then considered "Pascal's wager." "The reason I don't go along with that is the existence of God seems very improbable."

If a young, questioning Catholic approached her, Olivia would say to keep thinking about that topic. "But as far as her getting answers, she has to do that primarily on her own. I wouldn't want to sway her one way or the other, the way a lot of Catholics try to sway people." But she would want her children to have a religious background. "Going to church is beneficial. Then later, they can decide what they want."

PETE

Pete, nineteen, and his two younger siblings grew up in a northern city. His mother converted to Catholicism when she married his Catholic father, but they were "not very strict." The family did go to church "most Sundays," but when his sister and brother said they did not want to attend any more, "my parents really didn't like that but they didn't force us to go." The real source of Pete's religious upbringing was his Catholic elementary school. "They really drilled the point home. You'd come to class on Monday morning and there would be extra marks for telling the teacher what the sermon was about." His Catholic high school "wasn't as bad, but we had to take religion all the way through." When he was younger, Pete would have liked to be involved in additional religious activities, but was unable to because he lived some distance from the church and school.

In his case, he says, religious teachings "didn't sink in well. I was always pretty much questioning, like 'this is stupid.' When I was five years old I was pretty much just spoon-fed, I just took it as it came. But as I grew up, maybe by grade 5 or 6, that is when I started really wondering." Pete never did like going to church. "It was boring and a waste of my time. I hated getting up Sunday morning." He went along with the sacraments and confession so he wouldn't stand out from his classmates, even though "it was getting ridiculous." In general, Pete said, "I was the kind of kid that doubted everything. I don't know why. I guess I am different, I don't just swallow this stuff."

An enrichment program, beginning about grade 5, helped

Pete to "look at things differently. They wanted you to think things through." He did this and "I think maybe that is when I just slowly started to sway a different way." Pete remembers his first questions arising because "I always thought of the whole Catholic religion as, if you need something, you just pray. God will help you." However, when he found himself in a "bad situation," he would think "God's not helping me here. I just never felt fulfilled by what they said it offered."

Pete did single out a high school religion course in which he was intrigued by how other people thought about religion. "I really enjoyed that class." In another ("frustrating") class a fellow student got into a lot of trouble for saying things like "Jesus is a crock of crap anyway." Pete remembers agreeing with what he was saying but not the way he said it. "A lot of times I felt like we were getting fed this and it was all garbage."

He did try to talk with his parents about his questions, but mostly they "stuck to the Catholic position." They were aware that he did not like church, and Pete's father got upset about it if the family did not attend. "But I think he understood that if I didn't want to go he shouldn't force me to." Outside of this, his parents "really didn't notice much. I just kept it to myself." Only recently has he talked in depth about religion with his friends, especially with his college roommate.

Pete doesn't want to leave Catholicism entirely because it might offend his parents. But he does not intend to send his children to church, or to a Catholic school, and in religious terms does not consider himself a Catholic. Later in high school, "I just got sick of it and said that's enough. It's no big deal any more." However, Pete does harbor some guilt and fear about the religious changes which have taken place. "This is a big step, actually talking about it with others instead of just keeping it inside. It is a big deal."

Pete thinks it is highly unlikely that he would ever go back to the Catholic religion. "It just seems like it's a crock. I suppose that the church has changed a lot through the years, but it just seems like they always have this holier-than-thou attitude and they shouldn't. A lot of the values they believe in just don't sit well in my stomach." Besides, "I think everyone should have their own religion. I don't think that there is one simple path for everybody to follow. Everybody's different."

Traveling back to the time he was thirteen, the younger Pete would think he was now "some kind of weirdo." He would be shocked because at thirteen he considered himself "a very Catholic person." He would tell his younger self to be careful about all the things one is taught, "don't just let it flow into you and not understand it. Don't accept things at just face value. You have to go a little bit deeper than that."

Pete explains his departure from religion, when others remained believing Catholics, by referring to his reading and thinking about religion. "I don't want to sound conceited, but I guess maybe we [in the gifted program] were more intelligent, thought more abstractly than most people. I was always fascinated with literature, I read a lot of books. Different questions fascinated me. I didn't like to just follow things all the time. I don't know why."

In evaluating the costs of becoming an apostate, Pete reflected on his school years. "I am sad and maybe a little upset that I went along with religion in elementary school. I had a good time in elementary school, but now I'm saying I didn't believe it. I was blind to myself." Also, "maybe I am sad that my dad was so religious and I would have liked to have gone to church with him more."

On the other hand, Pete has gained a great deal from his loss of religion. "It takes a lot off my back. Whereas I used to have to sit through things, I don't feel I have to believe any-more. I'm happy to have it finally out that I don't believe any more. It is better now that I can find something for me instead of letting other people give it to me. I can look inside me and find out what I want and not what people think I should want."

If a questioning thirteen-year-old came to him for advice about religion, Pete "would have a lot of apprehensions because I wouldn't want to be like the Catholic church whereby I am telling him what he should do. I'd tell him to think about his doubts, maybe read into them a bit more and let him answer a lot of the questions. But I would tell him not to just keep swallowing everything, and maybe he should question his beliefs more. I would make sure that he did not feel that he was different because of his beliefs. You can't push your beliefs on anyone else, that's my main point."

OTHER INTERVIEWS

The sixteen cases just summarized, four from each site and four from each year, best illustrate the "typical" Amazing Apostates we found in our study, as well as a few "atypical" cases. We shall now briefly describe our other interviews, so you can see the entire range of persons we gathered in our net. As before, we shall change the gender of half these students to protect their identities.

Quince, a Catholic, began to lose his faith at twelve when his parents stopped going to church after moving into the city. Learning about the theories of evolution and the "Big Bang" in high school led to further doubts. Quince's parents

96

"do not want to know" about his religious views. Although at times he feels "I have failed as a Catholic," he said, "I could not go back. I'd be a hypocrite."

Rachel, raised a Mennonite, was troubled at fifteen by inconsistencies she found in the Bible, including the depiction of God in the Old Testament. By eighteen she had rejected her faith, explaining "I believe in thinking. I believe in explanation." Rachel's parents believe she will "grow out of" her loss of faith. She feels she has lost both friends and a sense of security, but would not go back without "proof."

Steve grew up in the United Church. He started questioning the divinity of Jesus at thirteen, and became an atheist at fifteen. "Who wrote the Bible? How does anyone know?" His father realizes better than his mother how Steve feels. "It would break my mother's heart." He misses "knowing what the point of life is," but "how can you make yourself believe something you don't? I'm sick of being fake."

Tina, like Kathy (above), was raised a Catholic, but was turned off at twelve by the sexism of a new priest. Also, public schools from age thirteen on gave her a non-Catholic perspective. For a while Tina had to assume her mother's role in the family when her mother became ill, and was unwilling to submit to her parents' authority afterward. They know she no longer believes, but have never brought it up. She cannot accept "blind faith."

Ulysses was raised an Anglican, but attended Catholic schools. Interestingly, he attributes his atheism to this education: "I felt it [Catholicism] was a crock. There really is no proof." His beliefs were further challenged when the Anglican priest in his parish sexually molested a child. Though Ulysses's parents are angry at his loss of belief, he responds, "I'm an individual. I'm entitled to my beliefs."

Vivian always resented having the Catholic faith "hammered" into her. She began to question it actively in grade 10 through world history and science courses. She came to see God as "like Santa Claus," and wondered how true the Bible is. "I'm the kind of person who needs proof. Why do so many believe?" Vivian's parents only recently realized this change, but have never discussed it with her.

Wendell became an apostate from an Eastern religion. At eleven, he wondered if God existed, and learning about Christianity put his own faith in perspective. "Is there one God or many? Is there even one God?" He ceased to accept his family religion at sixteen, partly it seemed, to fit in better with his peers. Wendell's parents respect his decision, and he still attends services for their sake.

Xanthe is another Catholic who left the church over its attitudes toward women. For a long time she "looked the other way, slanting St. Paul's misogyny." But her parish priest treated her questions as silly. She also spotted hypocritical Catholics. When Xanthe broke from the faith at age twenty, her father cried. She still feels guilty. "I tried to argue myself out of leaving, but couldn't."

Yves was also raised a Catholic. At age twelve, the theory of evolution led him to question his faith. As he got older, he rejected his church's "strict rules." Rome seemed corrupt, and Catholicism ethnocentric. By fifteen Yves was a "holiday Catholic," as are his parents now, who have accepted his change. "I'm a more knowledgeable person. I'd be missing a lot in the world if I still believed."

Zenia was reared in an ethnic Catholic community. She first doubted her religion at age twelve when prayers went unanswered. But she also found services boring, and said, "I didn't need someone telling me what was right and wrong."

Her parents' anger over her dropping the home religion at seventeen has lessened over time. "I found my true self when I left Catholicism. I get to pick what I like."

Al also hails from a Catholic background. At fourteen, he began to hang out with peers who questioned authority. They argued against Catholic teachings, and convinced him that the church's position on abortion, homosexuality, premarital sex, and divorce was wrong. Al's mother found his apostasy at sixteen difficult to accept, but he feels "freer. I'm a lot happier. I couldn't believe in what the church says."

Betty first remembered questioning Catholicism at seven when she could not see her guardian angel. Many questions arose thereafter, although she "always believed." Her parents were not religious, but her grandmother gave her a strong upbringing. When her grandmother died, Betty joined her parents in apostasy at fifteen. "Religion is a storybook. Religious people don't know the history of religion."

Chuck was raised a Baptist. At age ten, the congregation split over the choice of a new pastor, and his mother took him to church in another town for a few more years. He stopped going at fifteen, a year after she stopped. Chuck explained, "Born-again Christians are so narrow-minded," citing homosexuality as an example. Also, "I have a real problem accepting something I can't explain myself."

Dawn started doubting Catholic teachings at twelve, when she wondered if punishment would really follow misdeeds. She "ran an experiment" by cursing Jesus in her thoughts, and nothing happened. Other doubts soon followed, and at sixteen Dawn stopped going to church. Her parents reacted bitterly, but think it is "a phase." None of Dawn's friends knows she has ceased to be a Catholic.

Ernie was such a good Catholic when he grew up, that the thought occurred to him that he might be the messiah he heard so much about. However, on a family trip to his parents' Eastern European homeland, he was so affected by the suffering he witnessed that be began to doubt the existence of God. He then became more disillusioned with religious teachings. To this day, Ernie has confided in no one except the interviewer about his real religious beliefs.

Fay was raised in a very religious Catholic family. But in grade 10 a religion class got her thinking about contradictions in the Bible. The questions multiplied, answers were not forthcoming, and by seventeen Fay stopped thinking of herself as Catholic, though she does like some of the "moral teachings." Only her ex-boyfriend knows her real religious feelings. Fay thinks her apostasy might stem from her need to have explanations when others might simply accept teachings without question.

Gord was raised Jewish. At thirteen, the Bible "didn't make too much sense, compared to science." The death of a beloved rabbi and his replacement by a less appreciated individual pushed Gord further from his faith; he could never return to Judaism. "I would be upsetting myself to please somebody else and I wouldn't do that." Gord speculates that he might be more religious if he had grown up in a larger, more supportive Jewish community. Yet, "Religion is a very important choice, not a family or community choice, but just up to the person."

Hilda, raised Catholic, began to think the Bible was "pretty vague about everything" at thirteen. A Catholic grade 9 religion class stimulated further questioning. Now, "I don't believe in most of what is said." Hilda still considers herself a Catholic and accepts some teachings (e.g., she believes in Jesus, but not that Mary was a virgin). She is not sure exactly why she lost her faith. "I just don't take things for granted. I really like to do things on my own."

Ike was raised to be a "go to church every Sunday" Catholic, but in grade 5 a boy from a nonreligious family raised issues like "can being baptized be erased?" When his eyes were opened to the misery and suffering in the world, Ike had trouble believing in God and religion. At thirteen he stopped considering himself Catholic, but still regularly goes to church to keep his parents happy. He gets some consolation from "knowing that there are other people out there that have been in my situation."

Jane's Sikh family enforced strict religious and behavioral rules. She "believed really strongly" in the religious teachings until she was ten, when religious stories didn't make sense any more." Jane's mother could not answer her questions, but later her sister and friends were more helpful. By thirteen she no longer considered herself to be a Sikh, although her parents still consider this "just a phase." At eighteen, Jane is especially concerned about religious restrictions on women: "I don't think I've found anybody that questioned their religion the way I did."

Kris, nineteen, developed a strong sense of religion from his Catholic schools, but began to feel hypocritical going to Mass because the rituals "didn't really hold any meaning any more for me." He accepts some moral teachings, but is troubled by teachings on homosexuality, creation, and "the whole Jesus story." Kris still feels guilty about losing faith, but doubts he will ever go back: "I try to understand things." He feels he is now "a more tolerant person. The Catholic church is extremely intolerant."

Liz first questioned Catholicism when, in posing for a group picture at her first communion, a priest leaned on her heavily. It really bothered her. Other aspects of religion soon "became a joke." A favorite biblical character, doubting

101

Thomas, became "sort of like a role model." By fifteen, Liz no longer considered herself to be "Catholic" because she needs to look at things critically and come up with her own answers.

Murray still goes to church with his "strict Catholic" family when he is home on weekends, but remembers that even in elementary school he had begun to drift away from religion. He is the sort of person who requires proof for beliefs like the creation story, and this contributed to his apostasy, along with his interactions with nonreligious friends in high school: "I feel more secure in my own beliefs, but I feel less secure in which direction I'm headed."

Nancy is the third-oldest of nine children whose Catholic mother was the dominant religious force in their lives. However, stories of wartime suffering, and seeing children with terminal illnesses made Nancy wonder how God could let this happen. She did hang on to the image of religiousness until she was married at twenty-two, when she moved away from home. Nancy's mother still warns her that she will "go to hell" if she doesn't follow God, but she has no intention of returning. "I like things that make sense."

Oscar was raised in a very religious United Church family and was confirmed at fifteen. But almost as far back as he can remember, he did not accept religious teachings. "I was that pain-in-the-ass kid that was always asking questions. I never believed." He still goes to church sometimes with his parents, and also took communion last year "for the sake of harmony in the family." Oscar regrets "nothing" about being nonreligious, and would not offer any advice to a questioning boy since he "wouldn't want to influence him."

Pam remembers pretending she wanted to go to her Catholic church when she was younger, even though there was a battle raging in her mind as to the truth of what was being taught, as early as grade 2 or 3. She has since resolved the conflict by deciding to follow her own principles. The religious changes in her life have cost her "a bit of my parents' happiness," but Pam feels she has benefitted by becoming more open-minded and focused on generating her own strong identity and spiritual goals in life.

Quentin, eighteen, believed what he was taught in his "Protestant" church until he was about twelve, when he remembers wondering how the tower of Babel could actually have happened. Although his parents were quite tolerant of his questions, Quentin began to argue with them about going to church—he didn't believe the stories, and found church boring. He soon saw himself as nonreligious. Quentin believes it is his questioning, "cynical" outlook that distinguishes him from others who stay with their religion.

Rose's ethnic Catholic family was alienated from their church when the parish priest refused to marry her brother because his fiancée did not convert to Catholicism. Although Rose has other questions about religion (e.g., its role in causing conflict in the world), the church's stand on her brother's marriage was the main cause of her apostasy. She envies "people who are really religious. It helps them in their everyday things." But Rose is glad she left: "It has given me the sense that it's okay to question things."

Shawn grew up "surrounded" by Roman Catholicism. At fourteen he wondered why he should go to church, why there were contradictions among different versions of Christianity, and whether there was a God. Shawn did "a lot of thinking on my own," and sees his apostasy as "a natural progression." He regrets that this contributed to a relationship with his parents that is "not the best." But he has also gained. "I'm able to constructively think about things and I'm very open-minded."

103

As a child, **Trish** had been "more fearful of religion" than she was actually religious. At ten, she "had a terrible fear of living forever: I couldn't grasp the concept of eternity." She felt guilty and fearful about her questions, but persisted and was an apostate by fourteen. Trish differs from her (religious) brother, she thinks, because she must be honest with herself, and avoid hypocrisy. Her loss of faith has cost her "sanctuary, you don't feel the warm comfort of a community." But she has gained "freedom and a little bit of enlightenment."

NOTES

1. Anne responded with either a 5 or 6 to all of these items on the Religious Emphasis scale, where the highest possible score was 6. We shall highlight similarly strong emphases in other cases.

2. Direct quotations in these case histories are based upon the tape recordings. Usually they are exact quotes, word for word. But we have left out the "uhmms" and "hmms," "false starts" and "inaudibles" you usually find in a taped conversation. Also, we have sometimes changed what was actually said to put things in the context of a larger statement, or to disguise the identity or gender of the student.

3

An Analysis of the Amazing Apostate Cases

We shall now try to figure out the Amazing Apostates. Who are they? Where did they come from? How did they end up this way? In part, we shall study their scores on our survey instruments to draw their composite picture. But in the main we shall go through the interviews, topic by topic, and count noses. How many of the forty-six were females? How many were first-born? How many were raised Catholic? And so on, seeking the "pushes" and "pulls" that diverted the AAs from their parents' path, carrying them ultimately to doubt and disbelief.

SCORES ON STANDARD SCALES

Let us crunch some numbers, dealing first with the tests that defined Amazing Apostates. In terms of their religious back-

105

ground, their forty-six scores on the Religious Emphasis scale ranged from 48 (e.g., Gina) to the maximum possible 96 (Ida), with an average of 64.7, more than double that for the entire sample, 30.3. Compared with others, the AAs had strong religious upbringings.

Yet they had amazingly low scores on the Christian Orthodoxy scale, ranging from 26 (Liz) to 116 (Chuck) and averaging a mere 79.3. In comparison, "Neutral" on the scale is 120, and the overall sample averaged 147.5.[1] The AAs rejected all the tenets of the Nicene Creed. While they did not *very strongly* reject everything—the rock bottom possible score would be 24—we are sure that in almost every case their parents would say "they were taught better."

We also collected scores on the Right-Wing Authoritarianism (RWA) scale in the screening booklet. This scale measures the "authoritarian follower" kind of person (Altemeyer, 1981, 1988, 1996; see Altemeyer, 1998, for a discussion of the "authoritarian leader" personality). Such persons submit to established authorities more than normal, tend to attack others in the name of authority, and stick to social conventions more than most people do. Research has shown that "High RWAs" tend to be prejudiced, mean-spirited, fearful, self-righteous, punitive, and "black and white" thinkers who could easily fall for demagogues. They thus seem to be the people most likely to join a Nazi-type movement if conditions in their country deteriorate enough.

Scores on the RWA Scale can range from 30 to 270. Our Amazing Apostates proved decidedly *un*authoritarian, varying from 38 to 165 and averaging 93.7, compared with 123.8 for the entire sample. Persons who score in the bottom quarter of an RWA distribution have traditionally been called relatively "Low RWAs," while those in the top quarter have been labeled "High RWAs." Among our forty-six Amazing Apostates, one finds twenty-six Lows and four Highs.

In our 1995 studies we asked our screening sample to answer the twenty-item "Questions" and "Doubts" scales presented in chapter 1. As you would predict, our nineteen AAs from that year had many more questions (scoring 85.4 on the Questions scale, on the average) than did the sample as a whole (55.1). As you would also expect, they ended up with far more doubts (78.6 vs. 42.8).

Note how often their questions (85.4) became doubts (78.6). Remember back in chapter 1, when we saw that questions often were resolved in the general sample? Not among these people. They had lots of questions, and almost all of them became active doubts. That produced their apostasy.

VITAL STATISTICS

Gender

Twenty-six of our forty-six AAs (56.5 percent) were men, which is all the more striking because at both our universities, women constituted 58 percent of the screening samples. Males thus demonstrated a greater tendency to become Amazing Apostates. They also showed up more often in the ranks of the *un*amazing apostates in our data, i.e., the students from *weak* religious backgrounds who dropped the family religion. If you look around many churches on Sunday mornings, you will notice the men tend to be somewhere else.

A pile of scientific studies has verified that males are less religious than females, overall (e.g., Batson et al., 1993; Levin et al., 1994). So our AA results fit into this pattern.

Birth Order

Our AAs tended slightly to be firstborns (48 percent, including two only children), rather than second-born (37 percent) or "laters" (15 percent). If this proved generally true, it would refute the stereotype that firstborns are more likely to accept the parents' beliefs.

Age

As for age, most of our Amazing Apostates (61 percent) were still looking forward to turning twenty. Although the individuals described in detail (Anne to Pete) tended to be older, the median age of all forty-six AAs equaled nineteen. One student (Nancy) had caught up to Jack Benny at thirty-nine.

HOME RELIGION

You no doubt noticed that most (63 percent) of the AAs had been raised Catholics. This fact sticks out even more when we realize Catholics constituted only 29 percent of the overall sample. Why was Catholicism more than twice as likely as the other religions to produce Amazing Apostates?

We think the answer comes in two parts. First, to become an *Amazing* Apostate you had to come from a strong religious background. The mainstream Protestant religions in our sample (such as the United Church and the Anglicans) seldom inspired such child-rearing. Many Catholic families, on the other hand, gave their offspring a "good Catholic upbringing," often as part of an ethnic identification (e.g., "French-Catholic," "Italian-Catholic"). So more Catholics than Protestants (or Jews) *could* have become Amazing Apostates.

But these are only potential AAs. Why did they become *real* ones? Basically the church's stand on various issues, particularly those relating to gender and sex, alienated them. These alienating teachings caused the Catholic church to lose more of its "properly raised" children than any other religion. We suspect that many Catholic educators know all about this.[2]

AMAZING APOSTATES IN THE INTERVIEWS

We should acknowledge, before going any further, that not all of our forty-six AAs turned out to be amazing, and not all proved to be apostates, strictly speaking. In a few cases (e.g., Harry, Chuck, and Rose) the student ceased to believe after the parents broke with their church. You would have to be mightily bored to find that "amazing." Similarly a few of our AAs (e.g., Dwight, Gina, and Lance) said they still identified with their home religion, even though they rejected almost everything their church taught (including the existence of

God and the divinity of Jesus). In almost every case these were Catholics, and as Lance put it, "I was born a Catholic, and I can't change that." This identification seems based more on cultural factors than religious beliefs.[3]

We also had several cases (e.g., Ida, Nick, and Oscar) in which students said they *never* believed any of the religion in which they were so strongly raised. This may be true; after all, you do espy some disinterested youth in the pews on Sunday. But we have kept the "never-evers" in the study because we find it hard to trust that never-ever. Still, Oscar insisted that he questioned his mother about the nature of God at age three, "and I can't say I've changed much since I was three." Quentin's faith began to fade at seven, when he found the story of the Tower of Babel unbelievable. And Pat recalled wanting proof for beliefs as early as first or second grade.

The First Questions

Nearly all our AAs could remember the first question that arose in their minds about their religion, thus testifying to the importance of the event. Most reported that this grappling occurred at the beginning of adolescence, when lots of things began to happen. On average, that first question arose at age 12.5.

Many different "first questions" arose among these forty-six students, nearly all of them familiar if you answered our "Twenty Questions" survey in chapter 1. But a few popped up more than any others. The "tip of the wedge" for nine students sprang from the Bible. They found stories such as Adam and Eve, or Noah and the Flood, hard to swallow, or they found contradictions in the Bible itself. On a related note,

110

three other students said biblical disagreement with the theory of evolution started them down the road to disbelief. And four others began because of conflicts they noticed with science in general. Seven other AAs began their journey at the heart of the matter, wondering if God really exists. Several mentioned the parallel to Santa Claus: "My parents told me *that* was true, too. What was the evidence for God, really?"

If you want a "nuclear" cause of the amazing apostasy we uncovered, it originates with this issue: Can you believe in the Bible, and its story of the existence of God?[4]

Six other students, nearly all of them female Catholics, first questioned the sexism they perceived in their religion. We found six others who balked at the closed-mindedness they saw in teachings about homosexuals, or the validity of other religions. The "problem of evil" gave four others pause. Beyond that, we mainly found unique first questions such as Dawn's wondering why she was not punished when she cursed Jesus in her thoughts.

Insight?

If you compare the listing above with the averages for our "Twenty Questions" given in chapter 1, something may strike you as odd. The problems that came up most often in *most* students' minds (i.e., what happens to us when we die, the death of a loved one, or the problem of evil—arguably *emotional* issues) seldom came up *first* in the minds of budding AAs. Instead, the things that bothered them tended to arise in the realm of *ideas*. These in turn got little play among students in general. The validity of the Bible ranked close to last among the questions asked by the overall sample, and few reported spotting contradictory teachings.

To be sure some of the other "AA issues" came up widely,

111

such as evolution versus creation. But basically the Amazing Apostates of the future were working from a different page than most other teenagers were. They were examining the *truth* of their religion.

What Happened to the "First Question"?

Nearly all (80 percent) of our AAs said they had felt guilty about questioning the family religion, or afraid of what would happen to them for doing so—at either the hand of God or the hands of their parents. Nearly half (21/46), therefore, *never asked anyone for help* with their first question. They kept it hidden, and tried to work off its sharp edges by themselves.

What happened to the twenty-five who tried to get help? Most of them went to one or both parents; others asked their priest or minister. But in most cases (17/25), this proved unsatisfactory. The parents got angry, or cried, or gave the same "pat" answers the religion did, or told them just to believe. Clergy offered reasoned answers to the questions more often, but failed to convince. "I couldn't get a straight answer," said Chuck. Vivian spent two hours discussing matters with a priest, at the end of which the priest reportedly said, "It's good that you're asking questions, so long as it doesn't weaken your faith."

In most of the eight cases where the children found help, they went to their mothers, who gave them a gentle, sympathetic hearing—but not ultimately satisfying answers.

Insight?

Could it be that the more parents and clergy stress religion to a child, the more likely the child will feel guilt or fear when questions arise later? If so, the emphasis becomes self-defeating at this critical time, because parents and clergy *want* children to bring these questions to them, not hide the seeds of doubt. But the more times a child has heard that her religion has a hold on the absolute truth, the harder it may be for her to ask for help in reconciling cracks that appear in the absolute.

Breaking Away

Given that the "first question" was never answered satisfactorily, we would expect this tip of the wedge to drive an ever wider gap between the individual and the family religion. And as we have already seen, eventually all our "Twenty Questions" tended to arise in these forty-six students and became active doubts.

The students did not merely question, however; most of our Amazing Apostates discussed religion with their close friends at this time. But only rarely (e.g., Bill, Al, and Ike) did the friends *start* the questioning. It typically proceeded as a mutual groping for the truth. Yet the parents usually did not know this was going on during the years their children became apostates. They found out too late.

How many years did it take? Over three. Our AAs had broken with their home religions, in their minds, at age 15.9 on the average, at which point most of the parents realized their child had rejected the family religion. But they often did not know why, it seems, and frequently thought it was "just a phase."[5]

In five cases (Dwight, Gina, Olivia, Ike, and Quince) the parents *still* had no idea their child had "gone astray," as the apostasy was completely hidden. (In three of these cases, no one else knew either, except the interviewer.)

Obviously, then, the apostasy was still tinged with fear or guilt in some instances. To put a number to it, fifteen of our AAs said they still worried about going to hell, or falling out with their parents. Nevertheless, twenty-five of the forty-six Amazing Apostates thought it "very unlikely" they would ever go back to being religious, and sixteen said it was "unlikely." Only a few thought there was "a chance" they might return.

The "Back to the Future" Scenario

Understandably, fully half of our AAs said their former selves would be shocked (would not believe, or would be very upset) at the news of their future apostasy. (Some of these even thought that their younger selves, like Scrooge in *A Christmas Carol* after he has seen the future, would have vowed to change their lives to avoid such an awful fate.) Nine others said their younger selves would have reacted with lesser degrees of surprise. But fourteen thought they would have understood the transition, saying things like "I found church boring even back then," and "I was always one to question things."

Insight?

We found it interesting how often the Amazing Apostates distanced themselves from their past in the "Back to the

Future" scenario. After all, they were explaining things to their *selves*, not some stranger. But they frequently commented that earlier in their lives they had been "so naive," "unaware," "so simple," and "gullible." They typically laughed at how panicked their younger selves would have become at news of what lay a few years down the road.

We accordingly sensed the momentous discontinuity in their lives, one that probably still affected them every day, as they turned themselves inside-out from devout followers to disbelievers. Like their religious counterparts, they had been "born again."

Did a General Critical Outlook Come First?

How often did the apostasy arise from a *general* tendency to question things that just knocked down the religious beliefs along with everything else, like the youth counterculture of the sixties? This "youthful rebellion" hypothesis says that apostasy springs from a general critical attitude toward authorities and social customs. The critical outlook comes first, and religious beliefs are just one of the many pins bowled over by such an orientation.

You will recall we asked our AAs to write down, before the interview, whether they thought their loss of religious beliefs had arisen because they had become critical of many things. Only twelve of the forty-six AAs thought this described their transition. On the other hand, twice as many said the religious doubts had arisen first. *If* they were now generally critical of things, religion had made them so, they thought. (The other ten AAs could not say which had come first.)

Problems with the Parents

You may recall that the ages twelve to seventeen can be fairly tumultuous, with lots of door-slamming, storming out of the house, and sulking. Did the apostasy in these amazing cases arise from major crises in parent-teen relations, or broken homes, or severe problems with siblings?

Most (twenty-seven) of our AAs stated there had been no unusual problem with their parents during the time they were transforming themselves, sometimes adding things like "I was the perfect child" and "we were quite close as a family." The other nineteen came up with a wide range of troubles. Most commonly (six), some of the AAs strongly resented "unfair strictness" by their highly religious parents over curfews and adolescent activities. Three others had long-term blow-ups over their choice of friends. In several instances we saw signs of great resentment toward a sibling. But only two AAs had major teen-parent fights over alcohol or drugs.

If you perceive religious families as being closer than normal, and their children as more dutiful than usual, the data fit this stereotype. For example, only three of the forty-six sets of parents (Bill's, Harry's, and Lance's) had separated or divorced. The other forty-three apostates came from intact, two-parent families.

Having said this, we should also realize that in a few cases (e.g., Anne and Frank) the apostates may have had a silent ally in the family: a parent who was noticeably less religious than the other. The less devout parents never *encouraged* doubt. But their example in not attending church could have provided a model for the budding disbeliever. Still, this does not explain, for instance, why Anne and her brothers dropped their

116

faith, but her sisters remained devout. And such cases proved rare. Most of the time, both parents strongly believed.

Insight?

So, then, is amazing apostasy part of a general rebellion against the parents' values? Does it tend to spring from bad relationships with parents? Is it the children's revenge against parents they have come to hate? Do such apostates tend to come from unhappy homes? The answer would seem to be no in each case. In almost every instance the biggest problem the Amazing Apostates had with their parents arose over religion. The roots of the apostasy usually lay in the religious beliefs themselves, not some hidden underlying cause.

Costs and Gains

The solid majority of our AAs felt their apostasy had cost them a great deal. Most frequently (sixteen cases), they cited a painful deterioration in relationships with their parents. This commonly extended to others as well, as grandparents, aunts, siblings, and cousins now viewed them as traitors "in the grip of Satan."

Almost as often (twelve cases), Amazing Apostates noted they had lost their compass in life, "their answer to everything," and now had to wrestle with all the issues that their religion had previously decided for them. These students spoke of feeling isolated and confused; they had lost the comfort and security that firmly held religious beliefs can bring. Three said they now feared death more than before. Others missed the ritual of church services, the identification with a vast movement, or felt they had "failed to be a good Catholic." A few AAs reported they had lost nearly all their friends.

Nevertheless, all but three of the Amazing Apostates felt recompensed in some way. True, in ten cases the improvements included the fairly superficial "I get to sleep in on Sundays." But usually the gains appeared substantial. Most frequently, the apostates said that they now were their "own person," that they were freer, that they had begun to stake out their own identity. Nearly as often, they felt more objective, knowledgeable, and open-minded. They also commonly reported feeling stronger, with more self-confidence. But curiously, they almost never came right out and said they were happier, although all the above would seem to imply it.

WHY *THEM*?

Let us now seize with both hands the central issue in this matter: Why did *these* people become apostates, when almost all others from their background did not? For after all, whatever price they have paid, they chose their fate and continue to choose it. What drove them to such lengths?

One can find a clear enough explanation in their own accounts: They simply found it impossible to believe their religious beliefs were true. They usually did not leap to this conclusion in a flash; it took about three years of growing doubts. But as they said again and again in the interviews, eventually they could not make themselves go on believing what seemed to them false. They quit, as they often said, because they had no other choice.

118

It is not our role or mission here to pronounce traditional religious teachings true or false. But we should observe that the AAs did, in fact, have another option, which people from their background quite commonly select: faith. Religions usually teach their followers that some things have to be believed even if they cannot be proved, even if they seem to go against the evidence—even if they seem impossible. Charity may be, as the apostle Paul put it, the greatest of the cardinal virtues, but faith is so essential to the religious process that the word has become synonymous with religion itself, as in "the Lutheran faith." So the question looms, why could not these forty-six people "keep the faith" that their grandparents, mothers and fathers, and brothers and sisters staunchly maintained?

The AAs answered many times that faith was hardly a virtue to them, since it disconnects rationality. They also sometimes noted that religions have little use for faith when it supports beliefs in *other* religions. And as some of them put it, if it boils down to faith, how do you know which religion to put your faith in? Do not most people just assume they were luckily born into the right one? Most people have to be wrong then. Maybe they all are, they said.

But beyond that, recall what they replied when we asked them why they could no longer accept, and why they would not "go back to the bosom of Abraham." Anne said, "I don't like being told how you should interpret different readings. Why can't you make up your own mind?" Bill pointed out that "Those things aren't nearly as important to me as freedom of thought and freedom of expression. My father certainly is important to me but if it means me having to conform to something that I simply don't believe in, I can't do that." Claire could not be a hypocrite: "I have to be true to myself, I have to be honest. . . . I do not believe it. I could not make

119

myself believe it. I would not be true to myself. I'd be lying to myself." Dwight would not give up his lifestyle or his freedom of choice. "I decided what I wanted to believe in, not what I was forced to believe. I've seen both sides of the issue." And so on. Amazing Apostates seem highly committed to truth and integrity, so committed they will pay heavy prices to pursue them. Where did these values come from?

Insight?

We think they came largely from the religious training itself. Consider this: for all their lives the AAs were told their religion was the *true* religion, and they *had to live* according to its teachings. Were they not then being implicitly told that truth was a more basic good than even their religious beliefs, that the beliefs were to be celebrated *because* they were the truth? Furthermore, all the training in avoiding sin and being a good person "on the inside" would have promoted integrity. God knows all your deeds and thoughts. You have to be good and true, through and through. That's what counts.

If this teaching succeeded, it would produce someone who deeply valued the truth and had deep-down integrity. The religion would therefore create the basis for its own downfall, *if* it came up short in these departments. It may furthermore have added to its vulnerability by insisting that *all* of its teachings were the absolute truth. When the first teaching failed, in the mind of a devout believer, that put the whole system of beliefs at risk.

So what is different about the AAs, that they could do such a thing? They are, as a group, very bright. Twenty-six of them had been "A students" in high school. They often spoke of being among the top in their class, being placed in "gifted" programs, and getting high grades with little work. Fourteen others said they had gotten B's and B-pluses. Only three of the forty-six had been "average" students.[6]

Traditional religious teachings would "come up short" in the truth department more often in bright minds, *if* the teachings did not make sense. People disagree about that "*if*," of course. But all will probably agree that a personal history of being rewarded for "getting the right answer" will produce a greater drive for right answers, as well as a greater confidence in one's ability to work them out. Again, the religion would ultimately be subverted by the success of the socialization process, not its failure. The Amazing Apostate simply applied to religion what he was trained to apply to geometry.

So we would propose that while Amazing Apostasy is undoubtedly caused by many factors, two general causes stand out at this point. First, the religious training itself produces a strong valuing of truth and integrity, values children will not sacrifice for the family religion if it fails their test. Secondly, being bright may encourage some students to find flaws in their religion and make them more confident in their judgment.

ADVICE TO A BUDDING APOSTATE

We scored responses to our "budding apostate" question in two ways. First, did the Amazing Apostate indicate, directly or otherwise, that he would want a young questioner to end up an apostate like himself, versus leaving the decision up to the person seeking advice, whom he did not want to influence one way or the other? Secondly, would the AA's advice produce a two-sided search of the issue rather than a one-sided one that would—notwithstanding all the talk about people's right to decide on their own—lead to apostasy?

Only one of our forty-six Amazing Apostates (Quentin) indicated that he would try to turn a budding apostate into a real one. The other forty-five all said it would have to be up to the young questioner to decide. Many of them, as you saw in the case write-ups, went so far as to say they would never want to influence someone into following them. "It has to be her/his decision," they said over and over again.

The results proved almost as clean-cut on the issue of one-sided versus two-sided searches. Only three AAs gave one-sided advice that would favor doubt over belief. Thirty-six others outlined two-sided searches for the truth, often saying the budding apostate should consult a priest or minister, read the Bible, pray, or talk with parents as well as reading more widely, talking with atheists, and so on. (Six said they would give no advice, and in one case the matter remained unclear.)

So, just as they did not want to convince anyone to follow them, the vast majority of the AAs rejected biasing the search. They wanted the individual to decide things for herself, after considering both sides of the matter. They frequently volunteered, you will recall, that if the budding apostate decided to stay religious, that was fine with them.

HOW WOULD YOU RAISE YOUR CHILDREN?

Accordingly, we would expect the Amazing Apostates to give their own children a chance to become religious. Of nineteen

AAs (we only asked this question in the second year of the study), eight said they would send their children to church to learn about religion from believers. Eight others planned a more passive approach, letting their children learn about religion from grandparents, neighbors, and peers. They would not oppose these religious influences or try to talk their children out of becoming religious if that is what they chose. The remaining three AAs said "Don't know" or "It would depend on my spouse."

So overall, the Amazing Apostates do not seem determined to indoctrinate their children in atheism. They may have noticed from their own lives that parental wishes do not necessarily prevail, when all is said and done. But their openness is consistent with the decision they made for themselves, and consistent with freedom of choice and "searching for the truth on one's own, regardless of the consequences." If the AAs have not yet found the truth, they at least are proceeding with personal integrity.

So much for the Amazing Apostates. While every case had its unique features, we hope you agree that a fairly clear picture of the typical AA emerged from our interviews. Other investigators who think we missed the important questions, or misinterpreted what we heard, or just plain missed the boat entirely, can gather their own cases and correct our mistakes. (It will help to start with large samples to whittle down, for recall that only about 1 percent of our 4,264 introductory psychology students met the criteria for Amazing Apostasy.)

What do you think the other quarry of our search, "Amazing Believers," will be like? Will they prove psychological mirror-images of the Amazing Apostates, rejecting their family's *non*beliefs and shooting past the AAs in the opposite lane, heading to where the apostates just were? Will they have developed their religious beliefs on their own because they found their parents' nonbeliefs implausible? Will they also be driven to find the truth, whatever it is? Did their conversion start at the same age, and take about the same amount of time? Did their parents become upset?

We explore these issues in the following chapter.

NOTES

1. We have set aside our three Amazing Apostates from *non*-Christian backgrounds in this particular analysis, whose low Christian Orthodoxy scores did not spring simply from their apostasy.

2. To further illustrate the point, parents from two other denominations emphasized religion a lot: Mennonites and "fundamentalist Protestants." According to the composition of our overall sample, we would expect about two of our forty-six AAs to have Mennonite backgrounds, and two did. By the same reckoning, about three of the AAs should have come from fundamentalist Protestant homes, and three did (or four, depending on how you classify Ida). By the same reckoning, about thirteen of the AAs should have been Catholics, but twenty-eight (or twenty-nine—Ida again) were. So the Catholic church lost over twice as many of the youth it had succeeded in getting "raised right," as did other religions that also inspired a strong religious upbringing.

3. Perhaps we should set aside these students. But the ones who ceased believing in the family religion after their parents stopped attending church *could* have kept on believing. Isn't it significant that all that early emphasis failed to give religion deep roots? And a cultural identification with the home religion does not change the fact that our "Catholics in name only" were indeed Catholics in name only.

Scientists dislike discarding subjects who have met prearranged criteria, as this defeats the purpose of using objective standards. The next thing you know, you are pitching out "bad" subjects because they do not conform to your pet theory, thereby losing the greatest advantage of the scientific method: it tells you when you are wrong.

4. In this regard, Amazing Apostates resemble unamazing apostates (the ones who came from weak religious backgrounds). An examination of the latter's answers to our Doubts scale (see chapter 1) showed that ordinary apostates expressed much stronger doubts than most students on the following items: "The existence of God, an all-good, all-powerful supreme being who created the universe"; "Claims that the Bible is the word of God"; "Religious teachings often do not make sense; they seem contradictory or unbelievable"; and "Religious faith can make one 'blind,' not questioning teachings that should be questioned."

So these issues would seem to be the most common cause of dropping one's faith among our students. But of course it was a much harder thing for Amazing Apostates to do.

5. Is it just "a phase"? A definitive answer would require a long-term study. But other evidence suggests one had better not count on it. For one thing, you can always find apostates in parent samples, whose average age approaches fifty. In 1994, for example, 11 percent of the 447 Manitoba parents raised as Christians now said they had no religion. The apostasy rate among *students* that year equalled 19 percent, and remember, the parents had a firmer religious upbringing. So while we do not know when these parents became apostates, if you believe that adolescence and early adulthood pose the stiffest challenge to faith, it would appear most apostates remain apostates thirty years later.

A second line of evidence arises from a 1994 longitudinal study of 86 Manitoba alumni eighteen years after they started college. Among other things, they were asked how religious they now were, both in terms of beliefs and practice, compared to when they entered college. The response scale went from one ("Much Less") to five ("Much More"), with three indicating "The Same." Overall, there was hardly any change. The mean for religious beliefs equalled 3.18 and that for religious practice a nearly identical 3.17. Of course, some individuals became more religious on both counts, but nearly as many became less so.

Thus the common belief that we get more religious as we get older, perhaps even rebounding completely from a period of doubt, receives scant support. While teens undoubtedly go through "phases," apostasy seems much more serious and enduring.

6. We neglected to ask the question in three of the interviews. But there was no indication otherwise that the student had been outstanding.

You should expect to find good students at the university level. In this regard our two schools provide an interesting contrast. To get into the liberal arts program at Wilfrid Laurier University at the time of this study, a graduating high school student needed about a B+ average. Understandably, thirteen of the twenty-four AAs at Wilfrid Laurier University had been A students, and ten had been "B-plussers." But the University of Manitoba has lower admission standards (intentionally, to provide greater access to higher education). Still, thirteen of the twenty-two Manitoba AAs had been outstanding students, and four had mainly earned B's or B+'s in high school. So even when poor and average students could have entered our sample, AAs tended to be very bright.

We should add that both universities have lower admission standards for "mature students," some of whom turned up in our two nets.

4

Interviews with the Amazing Believers

This chapter will present what we learned from our conversations with the twenty-four very interesting "Amazing Believer" students. As with the Amazing Apostates, we shall present eight interviews from each university in detail, four from each year in Manitoba; (the only) three from Wilfrid Laurier in 1994, complemented by five from 1995 to match our total of sixteen AA cases from chapter 2. Brief summaries of the eight remaining Amazing Believer cases will bring this chapter to a close.

We shall once more systematically alternate the genders of our confidants, misidentifying half to protect everyone's identity, and make minor changes to the background information provided by these students. And again, quotations reflect things said during the interviews, but with some editing for redundancy, context, grammar, and the frequent hesitations and meanderings of conversation.

Art

Art never met his biological father. When he was five his mother married a Catholic, and a couple of years later a brother was born. Art's mother had initially given him an Anglican upbringing, but after marrying, they went to either a Catholic or a Protestant church, mostly for weddings or funerals, "occasionally on a Sunday but not very often." Religion was not very important in Art's family: "I was kind of taught that religion was something that you had to find for yourself. It was always in the background but it wasn't that emphasized." A few friends were religious, especially his best friend, who "came from a pretty religious family."

An important turning point in life came at age ten when Art's grandfather died. "That got me thinking more about religion, and because he had been very close to me, I started praying regularly, like every night." Some of his concerns revolved around the issue of death, but also, "I've always wanted to try and improve upon myself and be a better person." Art's interest in religion did not peak until he was fifteen or sixteen, though, when he "really started thinking about it on my own." He did disclose some of his religious views to his girlfriend at the time, but mostly he worked this through "just by myself."

One of the reasons Art kept his religion private was that he was concerned about the reactions he might get from others. "I worried about what some people might think of my views because my views are different from both my parents'. I'm just a worrier." As his views developed further, Art occasionally discussed them with friends, and was surprised to

128

find that they were quite supportive of his emerging religiosity. But mostly, "for information I would go to the library and look up different books." He doesn't know if his parents were aware of the changes taking place, because "I've never really talked with them about it much." But even if they had known, "it wouldn't matter to them." Art's parents today are quite aware that he is a Christian, but not Catholic. "It is just not an issue."

When Art was in grade 9, his family moved to a new town and he had some adjustment difficulties. "I started feeling depressed and stuff and I didn't go out much. I was in my room and watched TV and just thought about things. I found comfort in religion." He didn't go to church, however, because "I have my own beliefs, my own beliefs have comforted me."

Art has always thought of himself as a "Christian," and tried to follow the Ten Commandments. He read some "critiques of Catholic religion" and decided that he was not Catholic. When he was about sixteen, he began thinking of himself as Protestant, though he said he does not fit any particular denomination and he continues to avoid affiliation with any church: "You don't have to go to church. My mother taught me that it is something that you have to find by yourself. You can have organized religion to kind of guide you but I don't feel that they should be telling you that this is the only way. So, I don't really feel you have to go to church to be religious." Art now reads the Bible sometimes, and prays nightly.

Unlike many ABs, Art does not share his religious views with many others. Only a few friends know his real position on religion. But he is comfortable with his beliefs, feeling no guilt, fear, or regret. However, his religious journey is not over, and he thinks his religious views could change. "I am still working with some ideas." In spite of the fact that "I'm pretty firm in my beliefs," he added, "I'm very open-minded. I listen to what other people have to say."

If Art were to travel back in time and visit his nine-year-old self, he would tell him: "Just take it easy, think things through. Don't let anybody pressure you or tell you what's right and what's wrong. Make your own judgments. Be open-minded, though." This, Art feels, would not surprise his younger self at all.

There were "no problems with my family," and he did fairly well in school, receiving a mix of A's and B's. "I wouldn't say I was one of the best students, but I was above average."

Art acknowledged that his religiousness is quite unusual in light of his rather nonreligious upbringing, especially since his brother is not religious at all. He thinks his bout of depression contributed to his turn to religion. "I became religious probably because I was uncertain about my future at the time and I was in my room, and I would just think philosophically and just wonder." This gave him a "better sense of comfort. I have a feeling that no matter what happens, everything will be fine in the end."

When asked what costs might be involved in his becoming more religious, Art replied immediately "none whatsoever." The other side of the ledger, the gains, generated several ideas, including "a better sense of security. I often have a feeling that things will turn out better in the end. But I'm also a worrier, so that helps me get by sometimes." In a general sense, Art feels that he is "a better person for it."

Art would not go back to his less religious days "because they're my views, they're part of me now. I can't really throw them away unless somebody brings up a point or some kind of fact and I debate this fact to myself and then some of my views might change. I can't say that I would become less religious unless something really major happened in my life."

Art intends to raise his children the same way he was raised, "probably having the Bible around the house . . . and if you ever have any questions, then you can ask me or your mother. I wouldn't pressure them into anything." He would, however, be inclined to give them religious options in their lives, rather than nonreligious ones. This is illustrated by the advice he would give to a young fellow who was struggling with an inclination to become more religious. "There's so many different religions out there, stay receptive to them all. They all have good ideas, but just be careful and decide what's best for you."

BEV

Aged twenty when interviewed, and in her third year at college, Bev was the third of four children raised in a large city. Her score of 7 on the Religious Emphasis scale drives home the point that she had virtually no religion in her upbringing. Her parents "don't really have a religion. They're Roman Catholics, but it's based more on their nationality." They took their children to Mass at an ethnic Catholic church, but stopped attending when Bev was twelve after the death of a favorite priest. While Bev had been baptized and received her first communion in that church, she got little from the services, which were conducted in an Old World language she did not understand.

Bev's parents sent her to Catholic schools, "but not for religious reasons. They wanted me to become a lawyer or doctor," and these schools paved the way to a professional future, the parents believed. Bev developed a negative attitude toward all religion from this schooling. "They mixed religious belief with this drive to succeed, and it became very corrupt. What they were trying to do was very hypocritical. It angered me no end. I just shut out all the religion there."

When sixteen, Bev got a job waitressing at a posh restaurant. "Then *I* became corrupt. I came to money. I started going to bars all the time with my older coworkers. These people were heavy into drugs, which I never used but they used them in my presence." The restaurant itself also corrupted. "There's sexual harassment, there's blatant homosexuality, drug use, alcoholism. It's a modern day Sodom and Gomorrah." But Bev's coworkers became her friends, and she stopped hanging out with her schoolmates. Her escapades and abundant spending money gave her a certain "cool" image at her high school, "which I really loved."

At this point, a recent convert to Christianity named Mary also began to work at the restaurant. She did not fit in well with the rest of the staff, but slowly became friendly with Bev. However, they disagreed over religion. "I very slowly explained to Mary that there is no God."

Mary then got one of her friends, Steve, a job in the same restaurant. Steve "is a very handsome guy. Although he was very quiet about his beliefs, it was obvious that he was a Christian. He was so naive, pure, and innocent." He, more than Mary, changed Bev's life. "We never dated then, but he became an important tie to me. I saw how he lived, and his spiritual aspects." This led Bev to stop going to bars.

Steve went to a missionary school for a year, but he and

Bev wrote to each other. When he returned, Bev was in "a bad relationship with a guy who had gotten her back to drinking." She had a long talk with Steve and Mary upon Steve's return, and "it all became clear to me at once. I decided that Christianity was the right path to take. I started praying."

The interviewer suggested it sounded a little like what happened to the apostle Paul on the road to Damascus. Bev said it was not. "Steve had gotten me believing in God. But it was not 'reborn' Christian belief. That's a word I don't like, because it has a lot of negative connotations to it."

The relationship with Steve has since followed a tortured path. He has not reciprocated the strong romantic feelings that developed in Bev. But she became more and more involved in his (Mennonite) church in his home town. Bev also became an outcast among her old friends at the restaurant: "They knew that what they were doing was wrong in my eyes." But she has replaced them with new Christian acquaintances in Steve's home town.

Bev has considered herself a Mennonite for the past year. She attends Steve's church weekly, reads the Bible for thirty minutes every day, and does other devotional reading. She goes out to Steve's home town one night a week to talk about God and Jesus with whomever shows up in the local cafe. When she prays, "I used to pray for strength not to sin, to resist getting into the old habits of mine. But being such a strong Christian now, being so obedient, walking in such a straight path, I pray in thanks for all I have."

Bev's parents know their daughter goes to a Mennonite Church now, but they understand little else. She would tell them all, but they seem uninterested. They never pressured Bev to practice Catholicism. Steve suggested inviting her parents to a Mennonite service on Christmas, but they declined.

However, Bev has never felt any fear or guilt about becoming a devout Christian. She thinks it very unlikely she would go back to being a non-Christian. "I'm extremely happy right now. A lot happier than I have ever been. All my friends are Christians. I plan to marry a Christian. I don't date non-Christian guys."

Bev thought her sixteen-year-old self in the "Back to the Future" fantasy would not believe the transformation that has occurred. How would she explain it, then? "When you go through all the negatives, and finally you find some positive in your life, you feel a love that you had never felt before." She particularly felt this love from Steve's family. "They loved me more than my own family did." Bev had a definite understanding of what led her to become a Christian. "It was Steve. Mary too, to some extent. But Steve showed me perfect spirituality."

Bev said she was close to her mother, but not her father. Her adolescence had tumultuous moments. At that time, "I slept at home and that was it." Now her parents know her even less, she feels. She had excellent grades in school, until she started working at the restaurant. Bev's religious awakening has produced strain with some of her Catholic relatives. But the rewards have overwhelmed her.

Bev had recently encountered the situation of a young person asking for advice about Christianity. "I told him to listen to the words that Christians told him, but not to rely upon them. Instead he should read the Bible, because Christians can be corrupt. And who knows if I am right? When it comes down to it, you have to be an individual, and do it on your own. I'm not really interested in preaching. I used to hate that when I was an atheist. I'd become [this questioning person's] friend, and talk about religion when it came up."

CAM

Having become a Christian just six months before the interview, Cam was still somewhat excited about this new commitment in his life. The third of four children, he lived with his father after his parents divorced when he was eleven. His absolute zero score on the Religious Emphasis scale coincides with his observation that religion in his childhood was "nonexistent if not even a little negative," and he "really had no desire to go to church."

Cam felt like "a social outcast" all through elementary school because he "had trouble fitting in," but insisted this had nothing to do with religion. High school was a big improvement socially, especially because of his friendships with other Christian students. He managed to get mostly A's in both elementary and high school.

"I think that I've sort of been religious all my life. I just wasn't aware." Cam first began to recognize that he was more religious when he was about fifteen. He attributed this to the questions adolescents often ask about themselves. "You start questioning the world and where is my life going. And in questioning that, you wonder, what is my purpose in life and why am I here, and all sorts of questions like that."

Cam mentioned two other significant factors which might have contributed to his eventual religiousness. First, "When I was about six or seven, two grandparents died within a relatively close space of each other. That's the first intro to death that I had. So I began wondering about death, end of life, where do we go from there?" Second, in high school, a close friend of his became a Christian and "we just sort of compared ideas. He also discovered that some of his other friends were Christians, and they then talked about religion. These friendships, were very important, "there were bonds there, there was a trust."

Initially Cam felt guilty about his emerging religiousness. "There's so much responsibility involved in the whole idea of Christianity as far as the type of life that you are expected to lead. So fear of commitment held me back for a while. Also I felt, not ashamed, but uneasy going to church, because I knew I didn't know anything and I was surrounded by people who were raised in the church environment. I felt really out of my element. So for a long time he usually "stayed at home and was very internal." Through his struggles about whether to become a Christian, Cam did not go to anyone except his friends to talk about things. He also did some reading and he attended a "very multicultural high school," where "I was exposed to a lot of different things."

He got involved in a Christian Fellowship organization in high school, which provided "a networking system with other students at my school who are Christians who had common interests." Cam well recalls the day that he became a Christian. He was talking on the phone with a friend, having a "very deep meaning-of-life conversation." It was not unique or more meaningful than many other similar discussions, but something happened this time. "It just hit home that day. Everything clicked together and it made sense. It was just sort of an awakening. The time was now to stop all the procrastinating. Christianity was what I wanted my life to be about."

Cam refuses to think of himself as a member of a denomination. "I haven't chosen an actual church. I'm a Christian first." He has been attending a Baptist church recently, but is not sure he will stick with it because there are many other churches he wants to visit as well.

His parents are now aware of his church attendance "and my father really is not that happy about it." He attributes his father's negativity to religion to the fact that "he was raised in an environment where religion was really pushed on him and he wasn't really willing to accept it . . . he's automatically on his guard as soon as he hears religion." Cam's mother, on the other hand, is "passively supportive."

Cam talked freely about "a rough childhood," which put his religiosity in a somewhat different perspective. "Growing up was very difficult for me. I had a hard time fitting in, and I just had every single kind of problem that you could even think of. . . . Throughout my whole high school career there were many, many downs, many ups. It was very unstable, but religion was always stable. It was something that I could always go back to and find insight or comfort or whatever it was that I needed." These problems were compounded by the unreasonable strictness of his father, the difficulty he had living with him, and his mother's battle with substance abuse, among other things.

Cam struggled with his decision to become a Christian, but found consolation in his Christian friends. "Even in the first few months of being a Christian I wasn't always sure that I was doing the right thing and I needed a lot of support. That's really when my Christian friends rallied around me and made sure that I was comfortable. They were very, very supportive. It was really nice."

He tries to go to church almost very week now, participates in "devotionals" with a self-study group, and tries to "completely immerse" himself in Christianity. He has had some arguments with non-Christian friends, and has found himself defending Christianity in discussions about racism, homosexuality, or the "bad things" done by Christians over the years. But, "I'm not personally responsible for that as a Christian. I kind of feel bad that it happened."

Cam cannot conceive of himself leaving Christianity now. "It's been such an amazing change." He feels "reborn" and "I've evolved spiritually in such a way that I don't know that I could go back."

How would Cam explain the change in his life to his ten-year-old self, if he were able to travel back in time? "Well, in the next ten years you are going to be going through some pretty deep, heavy stuff. But you are going to make some serious realizations in your life as to where you want your life to go. Take charge of your life. There is more to life out there than just this whole earthly mess." The younger self would probably say, "You're wasting my time. Don't talk to me in your stupid religious psychobabble. Get out of here."

Cam has followed a very different path from his siblings. A sister calls herself a Christian but "she doesn't really live a Christian life." His brother is "very, very anti-religious . . . a hard-core atheist." Why did Cam become a very religious person when his siblings did not? He says he was never very close to his biological family. His Christian friends have become his "other family," and their support and encouragement made the difference. "Through them I have found a lot of the nurturing that I don't get at home."

Although he does not think that his religiousness has "cost" him anything, he pointed out that he no longer, for example, goes drinking with friends. "I don't really miss it now that it is gone, but it has restricted me in how I can relate with my nonreligious friends." When asked what he had gained, Cam responded, "Do you have another tape?" He mentioned security, knowledge, strength in faith, strength in purpose, ability to cope with adversity, new friendships ("social bonds"), and fellowship.

How will Cam raise his children? "Knowing that I'm going to marry someone who's a Christian, we'll probably raise them as Christians." He would accept it if his children later choose "not to go that route" because, although he wants to raise them "within the Bible as Christians, I also want to teach them to think for themselves."

If a thirteen-year-old boy similar to Cam came to him for advice regarding religion, he "would try to lead by example, and just share with him how I feel." He emphasized that he would not want to be "pushy," but rather be like a friend who helped him by being "always free with his view, but always very accepting of mine as well."

DIANE

Diane, age nineteen, was the second of three children, and the only girl, in a family living in a medium-size town. Her mother had a weak Christian upbringing, and her father stopped practicing his Lutheran faith many years ago. Consequently, while her parents provided "a Christian background," Diane said "up until a year and a half ago, I knew very little about religion." Her score on the Religious Emphasis scale was only 6 out of a possible 96. Yet she hit 212 on the Christian Orthodoxy scale, out of a possible 216.

Diane's religious awakening began at twelve, when her grandfather died. She had trouble accepting his death. She "had an inkling there was a God," so she prayed. "I was talking to someone, but it wasn't anyone I knew." She read books about prayer off and on over the next five years, and began to pray for help in difficult situations, but with no noticeable effect.

Then, when she was seventeen, she prayed for assistance as she faced a week of difficult exams. For the first time in her life, she did pretty well. She knew God had answered her prayers, she said: "There's a lot of skepticism because nobody else can feel it, but you know it when you're getting help. I've gone through years of exams before, and I was totally stressed out and depressed for weeks before. This time it had a totally different effect." Since then Diane has increasingly relied on prayer to get her through tough times. "My grandmother had a stroke, and my aunt had a bout with cancer and died. My mom is a total wreck. It doesn't affect me in the same way, and I can help people feel better." (But Diane began to weep at this point.)

Her parents had always told her she could make up her own mind about religion. They have neither hindered nor encouraged her movement toward Christianity. "They don't really care about it. It's my choice." Diane's father did object when she joined a fundamentalist congregation rather than a Lutheran one. But, she pointed out, there is no Lutheran church in her town.

Diane also disagreed openly when her parents said that the deceased aunt had gone to heaven. "How can she go to heaven? She didn't follow Christ, or follow any of the things written in the Bible about how you can get to heaven." Her mother insisted the aunt was with God, and would be waiting for them when their time came.

Diane provides a case of a completely self-generated conversion. No one brought her to Christianity, took her to church, gave her books, and so on. In fact, she did not tell anyone when she began thinking about religion. Her best friend, who noticed a change in Diane's behavior, only found out what had happened three months after Diane had made her decision. "It was kind of a soul-searching on my part. I knew I needed something else." Why? "I looked at people's lives around me. A lot of my friends, or my family, their lives are really distressing, with bad relationships, alcohol, drugs. It's really easy for someone to fall into that."

Diane was baptized at eighteen. She goes to church every Sunday she can. When circumstances prevent this, she has a private devotional service. She studies the Bible with friends every week. She prays often, and reads scripture every night. She thinks it unlikely she would ever give up her faith.

She has no regrets. "I feel I am a much better person than before." Did Diane ever feel guilty over pursuing a different path from her parents? No. They gave her the choice. She wishes they would come with her, but she knows she cannot force them. Did she ever experience fear over taking such a large step? No. In fact, she now feels less fear than ever before.

Diane thought her old sixteen-year-old self would have thought she was nuts. "Why would someone spend all that time doing something so meaningless?" To which she would tell her younger self, "It's not meaningless. It gives meaning to life. You can add meaning to other people's lives."

Oddly, while Diane thought she had always been a very moral person, her parents suspected her of immorality as a teenager. In this way, they are relieved that she is now "hanging out with a religious group."

When asked why she had become religious against all

141

odds, Diane replied, "I went searching. Most people don't because they think their life is great." She had seen lives heading for disaster, and this made her think. The interviewer then suggested that she had also seen death several times. Diane began to weep again, and said "Death is a scary thing."

Her turn to religion cost her one friendship. "I can't look at her now because of the choices she has made in her life." But Diane has grown closer to relatives who are more religious than her parents. What else has she gotten from becoming a Christian? "I got a new life. I really feel reborn." Diane also gained a very fulfilling relationship with "the greatest man I ever could meet." She had gone with another young man for two years. Then, on a camping trip with a large group, her old boyfriend "ditched her" for someone else. She was so depressed, "I said to God 'I give up looking for guys any more. That's your job now.'" Six hours later, although Diane is usually a very shy person, she approached a total stranger who was standing alone (another Mennonite, it turned out). They soon fell in love, and plan to marry.

The interviewer suggested that maybe life would be easier, better in some ways, if she went back to her old (non) beliefs. Predictably, Diane was not at all inclined to agree. "My old life really has no attraction for me now."

If a young nonbeliever approached her with questions about Christianity, Diane said, "I would ask her if I could pray with her. Because when you're starting out, you don't know how, by yourself. I would have to have an in-depth conversation first to find out what she's struggling with, what she needs help with. I would pray for a way to show her that someone's really listening."

ED

Ed (age eighteen) was the firstborn of three children raised on a farm outside a small city in Canada's north. His mother had been raised a Catholic, but had not been to church for many years. His father had no known religious beliefs. Consequently, the three children received virtually no instruction in religion. But Ed said he always "believed in God and stuff. We can't all just be here out of nothing." How had he realized this? "From TV." But he never prayed, and only passed through a church door three times in his life before grade 10.

When Ed was sixteen, his cousin took him to a weekend "Bible Camp" retreat at the Apostolic Church in town. His first comment in describing the camp was, "It was fun," not to mention dramatic: "There were these 'confessions.' There was this guy and he had drugs there, and he threw them into the fire, and said 'These won't ruin my life any more.'"

Once he got his driver's license, Ed and his sister attended these weekend retreats whenever they were held: "They made me feel good. It took up my spare time, gave me something to do." On a deeper level, "Christians seemed so much happier than others, and more understanding." Ed also had a prayer answered: while at a Bible camp meeting, the minister said "thank God for something, and then ask for something." Ed's girlfriend was away on a canoe trip, and he asked for her to return early so they could spend some time together before he left on a similar trip. Whereupon she came back five hours early. As he had made the request aloud, as part of the prayer service, many other campers were impressed.

Ed never felt guilty or afraid about becoming more religious. In fact, although they do not discuss religion, "my parents think it's really good. My dad's happy I'm a Christian. I generally have the same beliefs as my mom." Ed told his friends he was interested in religion, and they took him to their services as he "shopped around." While a few peers teased him, most of his friends were glad he was seeking Christ.

Ed has never "felt the presence of God," or experienced God talking to him. He has called himself a Christian since the age of seventeen, and was baptized in a Mennonite church. But he does not belong to any particular denomination: "I know what I believe, but I don't know what category it fits into." He reads the Bible every day, and prays occasionally for particular things, or help on exams. He goes to a Christian Youth Group every week when home, but hardly ever goes to Sunday services, partly because of a job. Also, "I have trouble getting up on Sundays."

While always believing in God, Ed feels he now knows God better. "He's always there, and he watches over everyone." When asked what he believes about Jesus, Ed simply responded, "He went through everything we do, and he died on the cross. I don't know . . ." he trailed off with a laugh.

Ed's fifteen-year-old self would just laugh in disbelief at the news he had become religious in three years. "When I went to the Bible camp, I just expected it to be a lot of fun, and nothing else." How would he explain it to his younger self, then? "I've seen so many things that I hadn't seen before. Like other teenagers who were Christians, too. I didn't think there were that many." Ed thinks it very unlikely he would ever go back to "my old ways."

Ed did not have problems with his parents during his adolescence. "My parents are really understanding. They gave me a lot of freedom. They didn't give me a curfew. Just said, 'Don't be late,' and I'd be early." We have a good family, and we're really tight." He pulled down "average" grades in most of his courses in high school.

When the interviewer asked what had "pulled" him to Christianity, Ed replied, "It seemed to change other people. I didn't really want to change, but when I saw that guy throwing away his drugs and stuff, I just thought that everything that was bad about me would leave." There wasn't that much bad about Ed. He had had a few drinks, he said. But "it was really neat how happy everybody could be."

The joy of young Christians particularly struck home at a "Youthquake" two summers before. "There were five thousand teens, and they were all Christians. And it was really fun. It took me away from all the peer pressures I get at home" to drink, do drugs, and not care about school. "It made me realize you can avoid all that stuff, and people will respect it." Ed had no regrets about his new life. Instead, "I feel good about things I do." Now that he is too old to go to the youth camps, he helps run the retreats as part of the staff.

The interviewer suggested "that some people find, when they have accepted Jesus as their personal savior, that it gives their whole life meaning that it didn't have before, that it explains everything." Ed replied, "I don't know that it has explained everything. I'm still confused about a lot of things." Such as? "Well, whether this Supreme Being already has our lives written out? If he has, then what's the use of asking for things? If it's not in God's plan, you're not going to get it."

Ed felt no temptation to go back to his old life. "I like it like this. But his new ways created stress with his (former) girlfriend: "Sometimes she's a Christian, sometimes she's not. She doesn't seem like other Christians at times." Ed tried to change her, and when that failed the relationship drew to a close.

Ed's first reaction to a young questioner would be to take him to church. But that might scare him. "If he didn't want to go to church, first of all, I'd take him to the Youth Group, so he could meet other people his age. I'd tell him it was good he was thinking about it." Whereupon the interviewer asked, "Would you want him to become like you?" Ed answered with the theme that had run throughout the interview: "Yes. I was happier before, but it has made me lots happier."

FRIEDA

Frieda and her older brother grew up in a family that believed in God but didn't talk about religion. The only time she was in church as a child was when she was baptized as an infant. She isn't sure, but thinks the family might have been Presbyterian. A couple of grandmothers are religious, and one gave her a children's Bible when she was younger, but they did not discuss religion. Thus, religion was virtually nonexistent in Frieda's childhood, consistent with her Religious Emphasis score of 4. Her grades were "mostly A's and B's" through elementary and high school, though with some lower grades.

Frieda thinks she "always had a basic belief in God," but by the age of seventeen, she was a much *more* religious person: "Going through problems as a teenager, people don't always have the answers. In the Bible they have a whole list

146

of different feelings, if you're lonely or anxious or anything like that. I used to turn to those pages and it didn't really make much sense to me. Then we moved, and when I was fifteen, I met some people who belonged to a church, a youth group. I had never been exposed to anything like that. They were going to Lake Placid, and I liked skiing, so I said sure. . . . They did some skits from the Bible and that really made an impact on me. Then I think I started reading the Bible more from there on my own."

She remembers reading in the Bible that "love does no wrong toward a neighbor, or something, and therefore love is the fulfillment of a lot. To me that was awesome, just that love was the fulfillment of a lot. I'd seen a lot of crime and everything, so I believed in that because in my heart that's what I believed." Although Frieda had read a bit of the Old Testament, "I never really got past Genesis. . . . In grade 10 I started from the New Testament and that's when things made sense."

At first Frieda's parents "thought it was kind of neat that I started going to church." But they lost their enthusiasm when it became clear that she was serious about religion, and she started going to go to church every week. Frieda herself felt "pretty good" about the changes taking place in her life, though she wished her parents would be a bit more understanding about it all.

The retreat at Lake Placid with other young people was clearly the pivotal point in her becoming a Christian. "That's when I accepted Jesus as my savior." However, "I didn't go to church for a year and a half. I just read the Bible on my own. . . . My life didn't really change much until about a year after I was at the retreat even though I had made the decision." Through this time she maintained close contact with her friends who became Christians on the same retreat, especially those who came from non-Christian backgrounds. "It was great to see that there's a lot of people my own age who had a faith."

Different aspects of the retreat itself convinced Frieda to change her life. For example, after watching a skit, retreatants broke into small discussion groups, during which one girl said she didn't know if there is a God. "My one friend stood up and she was very emotional about it. She wasn't angry or anything but just really moved by it and definitely standing up for her belief in God. That really moved me because I'd never seen anybody taking it so personally."

Also, Frieda was not very happy about her lifestyle before she became a Christian. "When I moved here after the whole drinking thing with the kids, it didn't seem like my idea of fun. I think there's a lot of things in my past that I was guilty of and just felt that in my heart and definitely knowing there was forgiveness for that."

Frieda was baptized at a Baptist church after her decision to become a Christian, though the earlier retreat had been sponsored by the Pentecostal church. "I go to a Baptist church right now. But I have lots of friends from different denominations . . . it isn't so much a relationship with the church, as with God." She now thinks of herself as a religious person (no denomination), goes to church every Sunday, reads the bible, prays regularly, and gets together with some other people in her dorm to pray and sing.

She does not talk about religion with her parents or her brother much, at least partly because she believes they would fear that she was being manipulated or exploited by religious groups. "This would cause conflicts with them." In fact, aside from her friends, no one really knew the extent of the change in her life. But she has no regrets about becoming much more religious. And although Frieda allows that "anything's possible," she thinks it is very unlikely that she would ever return to her less religious state. "I would definitely, definitely hope not."

Why not go back to her previous life? "I know God personally and I wouldn't go back for anything. My life has changed for the better. . . . I don't see any reason, and I wouldn't want to go against God's law and his standard." Frieda says her children will "definitely" get a religious upbringing. She looks forward to "having the opportunity to bring them up in a different way than my parents did . . . I can offer my children what I have found. I think that's better."

When she stepped out of the Delorean and met her fourteen-year-old self, Frieda would tell her that everybody is searching for something, we have that "vacuum" to fill, and "if you don't have God, it's pretty lonely. I definitely believe there's a heaven and I believe the only way to get there is by the death that Jesus did on the cross, and so I would definitely encourage myself to seek after that." The fourteen-year-old Frieda would have responded pretty negatively to all of this, being shocked by the change in her older self.

Though there was never any serious conflict between Frieda and her parents, she does admit to conflict with her brother ("we're just different people"). However, "I guess there's more conflict over this past summer, just with me being baptized."

Frieda did not believe she was unusual in her religious journey. "I don't know, I have a lot of close [religious] friends whose parents aren't Christians. So to me it seems . . . not so much out of the norm." Therefore, she did not offer any explanation for why she might be "different";

rather, she simply reiterated that she is "thankful and I definitely pray for my family."

There were no costs involved, as far as Frieda was concerned. In terms of benefits: "I don't have to spend eternity in separation from God." Also, "it's a better way for me."

Frieda would counsel a thirteen-year-old girl looking for advice about religion that "the only way to get to heaven is through accepting Jesus . . . you have to accept that in your heart by faith. I'd encourage her to have a relationship with God."

GIL

Eighteen years old at the time of the interview, Gil and his older sister grew up in the outskirts of a middle-sized city. His mother and father came from different religious backgrounds—Gil did not know what, specifically—which prevented them getting married in either church. So they joined a third church—also unknown to Gil—just for the ceremony. Obviously, religion had little importance in his family: he entered a church twice during his childhood. He only had one friend who was religious, and this friend took him to a church-related boy scout group twice. Beyond that, Gil had no contact with religion for almost all his life. He recalled having no religious impulses or "hints of God's existence" for all that time.

When he was sixteen, he began dating a girl whose father was the pastor of an evangelical church in a nearby town. "I started going to her youth group, and met a bunch of people there. And I talked with her over the phone, and with her dad when she couldn't answer the questions." What kind of questions? "Oh, we talked about Adam and Eve and evolution. And the Commandments, and what was wrong and right. We talked about heaven and hell." And he fell in love with her.

The interviewer asked Gil if his questions sprang from a yearning to know answers about life, a desire to connect with something more powerful. "Before I knew her, I really didn't care. I guess it filled a hole, one I never realized it was there. But it gave me an understanding of things I never had before."

Gil never felt that he was betraying his family by pursuing religion. His mother noticed a change. They had argued a lot over the years: "When we get in fights, we don't stop. Everyone wants to get the last word in." But one day I never said anything. I just agreed with everything she said. And his mother later put a message on his desk saying "You're helping me to see things." Gil had always been on good terms with his father, but they were not close. Both his parents liked his new girlfriend, but did not know the effect she was having on his life.

His growing religious zeal did not lead Gil to get baptized. "It's more something that is just knowing and accepting. It's just a feeling, not something I'm going out and doing. It makes me a better person. It makes me want to go to heaven instead of hell. It makes me want to do good things." But surprisingly, Gil did not know which religion his girlfriend belonged to. "I think it's Catholic." Told by the interviewer that was highly unlikely, Gil said "I didn't go into names or anything like that. That really didn't interest me. Probably if I heard the name, I would know it."

Asked in what ways he is now religious, Gil said, "Praying. Usually before bed. And the way I treat people. I treat them the way I'd want to be treated." But he does not read scripture regularly, he does not go to church, he is "not a member of anything."

Only a couple of Gil's friends, themselves religious, know about his new beliefs. When the interviewer asked if his parents would know his answers to the Christian Orthodoxy scale, Gil said, "I don't think they really know. It's not that they don't care." But his religious beliefs are invisible to most people. He felt no guilt or fear over "giving up the family tradition of being nonreligious." He thought it very unlikely he would ever go back to those ways.

If sent back to the time when he was fifteen, to confront his former self with his Christianity, Gil believed his younger version would not believe the change. "It wouldn't seem reachable." He was too involved in other things to get serious about religion. How would Gil explain the change then? "I met this girl. . . ."

Gil always did his homework, but just had "pretty average" grades in school. Once he became religious, however, his grades went up and he made the honor roll in grades 11 and 12: "I started writing things down. I had a plan. I knew what I wanted to do in life, and I did it."

When the interviewer asked him what would have happened if he had never met his girlfriend, Gil gave two answers: first, "It's hard to say. I never realized anything until I sat in Youth Group and listened. If I hadn't gone to Youth Group, I don't know if it would happen. A lot of the songs reached out and got to me. They were modern, they made you want to sing them. We went over the words, too. They had neat meaning." Second, while the relationship with the girlfriend has ended, the conversion has endured. "She was changing. She was rebelling against her dad, because she wasn't enjoying herself. She had so many commitments with the church. She was forced to go all the time, even to the Youth Groups. Now she is pretty screwed up. She smokes, she drinks a lot, she's into drugs. I tried to stop her, but there was nothing I could do." The relationship ended by mutual agreement some months ago. But Gil still goes to the Youth Group, and is still close to the parents of his former girlfriend.

Becoming religious had cost Gil nothing. On the plus side, "It makes me take time to think about things. It adds another topic to talk about with my friends. It gives me someone to tell my problems to." Gil knew God was always at the other end of the line, listening.

The interviewer then played the devil's advocate (literally), and asked Gil why he did not go back to his earlier ways. "You were happy then, weren't you?" Gil responded, "I thought I was. But I think I'm a better person now. Happier. More of my thoughts are together, and not all over the place."

Suppose a young person with no religious background began to wonder about religion, and came to him for advice. What would Gil say to him? "I would tell him to talk to a priest or a pastor. So he would know his feelings." Were there other people he should talk to, or things he should do, things he should read? "I never really read anything, except for the songs. I never talked to anyone." Suppose this young person, after talking to clerics, decided not to become religious? Gil responded, "That would be his decision. No one should be forced to believe."

HEATHER

"We've never attended church as a family. Really, religion is not a part of family life. We just don't talk about it. We've been raised with the same kind of morals and values as other people, but I don't think religion ever played a part." Heather, nineteen, and her younger sister clearly grew up in a very nonreligious environment in their small town. It is no wonder her Religious Emphasis score is just 6.

Heather was intrigued with the concept of God when she was younger: "I've always wondered about God. I had heard about God, but God was not really in my life. I never really thought about what it had to do with me or with the world." As she grew older, Heather "became more aware of religion." By the age of fourteen, she decided that she wanted "something to believe in—'why am I here?' type of thing. So I started looking for a reason and that's when I started exploring different religions. I think I was at an advantage because I haven't been baptized and I haven't been exposed to religion, so I take the broad spectrum of religions with an unbiased point of view." God and religion seemed to supply the answer to Heather's "why am I here?" question.

She did not share her religious views with anyone else as they developed. "I sort of did this off to the side. I never told anybody, probably out of fear about what they might think. I didn't want to seem weird or different from anyone else." She finally did summon enough courage to ask some religious neighbors if she could go to church with them, and they were happy to have her tag along. "I was feeling out my possibilities to see what I liked." Then she simply showed up at a neighborhood church on her own. Heather's parents, she assumes, thought she was "just curious" and did not realize how serious she was becoming about religion.

In many of our Amazing Believers, the influence of friends is important, but Heather does not think this was the case for her. She read "two or three books from the public library" and was impressed with the depth of people's beliefs that she read about. But basically, she says, she figured things out on her own, and started believing.

Heather is also unusual among our Amazing Believers in that she sees herself as still in transition. "I still believe in God now, and a lot of the teachings. But at the same time there is a lot of conflict, especially when you look at the creation versus evolution issue. I don't know. I'm starting to move more toward logic now, so I'm wondering if it was maybe just a phase through my teens." The night before the interview, Heather had a deep conversation with her roommate, who is an atheist, and thought the roommate made some good points. "It's hard because I still *want* to believe. I don't want to think I'm here and then I'm dead and I'm gone."

Heather does not identify with any one religion, but rather has developed her own personal views. "I don't attend church regularly. I take a lot from different religions, and sort of compose in my own mind what best suits me." Since the age of fifteen, she has considered herself a Christian, but does not attend church regularly, rarely reads scriptures, and prays just "once in a while." Her parents now know that she believes in God, but "I don't think they realize anything beyond that." They are not upset by what they do know about Heather's religiousness. Nobody else knows what she really feels about religion, either.

While Heather feels no guilt about her beliefs, she is fearful about "what is going to happen in the future. If I stop believing, what is going to happen if logic takes over from religion?" She thinks it is unlikely that she will ever become a "total" nonbeliever again, but "I might have to combine beliefs, you know, like logic and faith. Maybe I will have to redefine what I believed in the past to come up with a better belief that suits me today, but not totally abandon my religious beliefs."

Heather does not think her twelve-year-old self would be surprised to learn how she has turned to religion. "When I was twelve, anything was possible." Asked to explain the change in herself, Heather reiterated her need to make sense of, and anchor, her life. "I needed something to believe in. I needed a reason, something concrete, something stable in my life."

Encouraged to explain why she became religious when most people from similar backgrounds do not, Heather first pointed out that her parents did not teach *against* religion. Also, "I have always been the type of person who totally goes away from the group. I like to search things out on my own, do things my own way." She also reflected on her early social experiences. "During public school I would do my own thing. I didn't have a lot of friends, whereas my sister, she had tons. So I think she tended to follow the group more, but . . . I didn't. I didn't have a lot of influence from peers, so I tended not to think the way they did."

Heather has no regrets about becoming religious. She has benefitted from the change because her research and the development of her own beliefs has given her "more respect for the church and people. I have respect for all religions. I'm not biased toward any. I'm at an advantage because I have a better understanding of people and maybe the world. That's a big benefit." Also, she is a happier person "because I believe there's someone out there watching over me and everything will be okay."

She cannot consider returning to nonbelief. "I think belief makes my life more simplistic. It's less worry to believe that we've been created and put here for a reason, than to worry about, well, if there is no God. Why am I here? All those questions will become unanswered again, and I don't think that I've answered a lot of questions. I would not want to go back to a period where I'm uncertain about certain things."

Heather intends to raise her own children "kind of like the way I was raised. I liked that I wasn't baptized. It was basically up to me. I don't think I'm going to press any views on my children. I'm going to instill the same good morals and values that all parents should, but I'm not going to sway them in one direction or another. I may say I believe there is a God. If I want to go to church, fine, I'm not going to make my children go to church. I might take them when they are younger, but as they get older I'm going to say, okay, it is up to you."

If a thirteen-year-old girl came to her for advice, Heather would "definitely say what I did, I think is good. Research your religions, visit as many churches as possible, talk to people who are involved with religions, whether it be members of the church or the ministers. Just talk to people, read books, do all you can to get as much information as possible, so you make the best informed choice."

IVAN

Ivan enrolled in college at age twenty-five as a mature student. The youngest of eight children, he had grown up in a small town. His mother had never practiced the Lutheran faith into which she was baptized, and his father had not even been baptized. The family never attended church. Ivan went to Sunday School for a year when ten, because other kids in his town had been proselytizing, but he found he did not care for it. Still, at times he felt "a little bit left out" when his peers took part in religious activities together that he could not join. This happened often because his mother had him attend Catholic schools for academic and "discipline" reasons. But he never prayed and did not believe in God.

Yet at age twenty-five Ivan earned a score of 215 on the Christian Orthodoxy scale, just one short of a "completely believing" 216. His slow, painful conversion began when he was twenty and working full-time after finishing high school. Some acquaintances convinced him to go on an out-of-town Christian retreat for a weekend. "It sounded like fun. I more or less built friendships there. I didn't concentrate on the religious aspects of it."

Ivan explained that he "was at that age when everyone wants to go out and party. I really didn't think much about the retreat afterwards." Instead he picked up again with friends who would go out drinking together and stay out late. Then a good friend went to a Catholic Bible camp, enjoyed it, and brought Ivan to the next one. For some reason, the priest running the camp asked Ivan to serve as a counselor during the session. Ivan got "a spiritual high" from this experience, and that led him and his buddy to do four or five more weekend retreats. "But each time we'd come back to our jobs, start drinking again, and carry on like before."

Eventually Ivan got into trouble with the law. "It wasn't anything major, but it was alcohol-related. I went to a series of parties one night, got rowdy, and was evicted. Then I went back and broke some windows and got arrested." This made

Ivan stop and look at where he was going. He cut down on his drinking, and some months later went again on a weekend retreat. For the first time he prayed for himself. "Before, I never thought I had any problem," but now Ivan knew he needed help.

For a while, Ivan's parents, while they are not against religion per se, viewed his retreats and Bible camps with suspicion. "They saw that I was getting serious, driving two hours to get to these places. It seemed like there was something there controlling me. This was partly because there are some secret parts of the retreats that we're not supposed to talk about. You don't want to tip off people before they go to a retreat themselves. But my parents worried I was getting into some kind of cult." Now they are glad he has become religious. "I don't get drunk and into fights."

Ivan thought about religion for two more years, and was baptized a Catholic when twenty-four. He attends Mass most Sundays, and prays from time to time (usually for his father's health). He does not read scripture or participate in Catholic organizations. He feels his religion shows up "in my general attitude. I try to treat everyone fairly, equal. I don't judge others." Ivan's fellow workers will have noticed he does not swear as much, and is quieter. But he does not "make a show" of his religion or try to convert others.

Ivan thinks it is very unlikely he would ever go back to his old ways, at which point the interviewer used the "Back to the Future" scenario to revisit the eighteen-year-old Ivan: what would he think of the change time had wrought? Ivan explained that at that age, he was "a party animal," and into heavy metal music. So he would be stunned at the news of his impending conversion, and would probably say, "Get the hell out of here." Ivan would explain his new outlook thus: "I saw the change in myself, between when I drank and when I didn't. The friends I made at Bible camp seemed easygoing, more relaxed. Bible camps were an 'up,' and partying brought me down."

When asked about his adolescence, Ivan said he always got along well with his parents. But they worried about his drinking and driving afterward, during his "party years." He had gotten "pretty good" grades in high school: A's in English, and B's in his other courses.

When pressed for an explanation of how he had gone against his background, Ivan attributed the development to "influences outside the home. Close friends I made on the retreats." A sister had converted to Anglicanism ahead of him, and "now I have something to share with her."

Ivan has no regrets about becoming religious. On the contrary, besides the obvious improvements in his health and behavior, "After I quit drinking, a girl I knew saw the change in me, and she became attracted. The feelings were mutual, and we started dating. Now we're getting married next year."

"Why wouldn't you go back to your old life?" the interviewer asked. "Church wouldn't complicate your life, you could sleep in on Sundays, you could go back to having the fun that you used to have before. You said it was very unlikely you would go back, but why?" Ivan answered that if he did, he would lose all he has gotten recently: "As a direct result of giving up drinking, giving that up to God, God gave me my fiancée."

If someone came to Ivan for advice, a young man who had been "something of a party animal during high school," but who now was beginning to wonder about religion, what would he say? Ivan answered, "I would tell him to cut down on his drinking. I would tell him my story. Then I would definitely try to get him to a Bible camp, or some other program."

Ivan and his fiancée plan to raise their children as Catholics. He feels a religious upbringing will give them an "outline" of how to be good, how to avoid the troubles that could have swamped him.

JILL

Jill, twenty-one, had virtually no religious training when she was growing up. Her parents divorced when she was a toddler, and she was raised by her mother. "My mother wasn't a churchgoer and so I wasn't either." She did go to church a bit when in "junior high school, and that was because a lot of my friends were involved in a youth group there. That was mainly for nonreligious reasons, for athletics and social environment. It wasn't a religious sort of experience." But when she was about eleven, Jill "began to realize there is more out there beyond the school boundaries. It was probably as a result of the influence of science in school, teachings about creation, how various things were formed. I've always had a problem with science. I can't accept a lot of scientific information. The religious beliefs I stumbled into were just more believable. I'm not saying they were more correct or any more accurate. Just for me, at that time, they made more sense." Jill felt no guilt or fear about her emerging religious beliefs, and did not approach anyone else to discuss them. "I've never been an extroverted person who has asked a lot of questions and imposed myself on other people."

Jill's mother became aware of her interest in religion when she started going to a youth group at the age of thirteen or fourteen. It was "fine" with her that Jill was attending a youth group. Even today, although her mother has a general idea of her religious views, essentially no one *really* knows Jill's personal feelings about religion. She thinks it unlikely that she would ever go back to her nonreligious views.

When the interviewer pressed for further experiences or thinking which might have led Jill to become more religious, she mused about some problems she had during her teens. "I would say just growing up. You go through that adolescent stage when you perceive you are different and don't fit in — alienation, isolation, and all those sort of things. It was more a heightened awareness of how my life was different from the other kids."

From the age of about fifteen, Jill has thought of herself as "Christian," even though she has "never been formally introduced into the Christian faith, or baptized." "But I don't consider myself to be a stereotypical Christian, a regular church-goer. The limited church experience I did have was not one that I would like to go back to. It was not the church or the religion, it was more just the people involved. I found church very isolated, very cliquish. . . . I sort of stuck out like a sore thumb. I just didn't like the politics of the organization."

She does pray, and reads the Bible "on occasion, not so much for everyday comfort or because of guilt, but more because I'm very interested in literature and the Bible is always the influence on Western literature. I look at the Bible as more helpful in terms of understanding the transition from two thousand years ago to the present."

Jill's fourteen-year-old self would not have anticipated the religious turn in her life. But she would not have been surprised because "as far back as I can remember, I have been the sort of person who believes what she sees and learns from experience, not so much from parental influence or from societal influence." Further discussion revealed that, as an early teenager, she was looking for a way out of personal problems: "The fourteen-year-old Jill was very confused, very angry, very naive, a bit misguided, and very spiteful a lot of times. She had a lot of energy, and didn't know what to do with it. I didn't know how to do what I wanted to do, or how to get there."

The interviewer responded, "I think I understand the confusion, since you were trying to sort out a lot of questions in your life. But why was the anger there?" Jill replied, "Just the experience of adolescence. It was very alienating and isolating, it was a very, very difficult time, a very confused time, a very lonely time. I was angry because I didn't know what to do with all those emotions and feelings. You tend to bottle things up and become angry and spiteful. There was anger, confusion, naivete, and ignorance." Jill admits to some conflict with her mother, but says, "I can't think of a time when I was actually angry with my mother. I respect her too much."

Asked to explain her life path, compared to that of others who remain nonreligious, Jill said: "From the time I was a child, I always believed that my life was a clean slate, an empty page. There weren't any predisposed ideas, events, actions on that page. It was up to me to fill the page. I think a lot of people that I know who are not religious as a child and who are not religious today—it is not so much that they have rejected religion, it is more, I think, they just don't feel religion would help them. I tended to explore different options, different ideas, and what fit for me was what I retained."

Jill feels there have been no costs in becoming more religious; on the contrary, religion has helped her a great deal:

163

"I think I got over a lot of the adolescent confusion, anger, depression. That was a big help to me. I'm not saying religion is the end-all answer for me, but it went a long way in helping to sort through my maturity and my development. It was more of a personal journey. It helped me through a lot of difficult times, to understand things better. It made me realize that the world doesn't revolve around me."

Whereas some of our Amazing Believers said that religion provided them with a set of guidelines for living, this was not true of Jill. "Religion does not constitute a set of guidelines, a framework, a set of strict rules for me. I don't even know most of the sort of traditional rules you are supposed to abide by. I don't tend to work well in a structured environment."

If she has children, Jill hopes "to raise them the way I was raised, without much forced authority, forced views. I would like to let them decide things for themselves, have them grow up to be individuals. I don't attend church now, so I don't think in the future I will be a regular church-goer if I become a parent. I don't know if my views and opinions are the right ones. They are what works for me, what helps me get through the day and get through life. I've always been afraid of having too much influence on my children, shaping them to be versions of me or what I would like to be.

Similarly, the advice Jill would offer to a fifteen-year-old who was thinking about religion would not direct her to religion. "I would advise them to look at themselves, look inside, not worry about the outside world. Don't get too involved in outside interference, organizations, parents, whatever the case may be. Look within yourself and see if you can't find some sort of idea of where you are headed, what you would like to do. What you believe is true and don't be afraid to be different if you want to live your life differently. Most people already have the answer within them, but for whatever reason it's not brought out."

KEN

At forty, Ken is one of our oldest interviewees. He was the second of five children who grew up in a moderately sized city. One set of grandparents attended the United Church, but "all we ever heard of church was who had a new hat, who fell asleep in church . . . there was no context of a message. It was a social activity." Ken's other grandparents did take him to their Baptist church on Easter, but there was virtually no other religious activity or discussion in the family. His lack of religious upbringing did not make him feel out of place, however, since his school friends also tended to be nonreligious.

Ken says he "always did believe in God" and considered himself a Christian in spite of his nonreligious background, but in his early teens, a comment by a friend that he (Ken) was *not* a Christian caught him off guard. However, nothing much happened until he was eighteen, when a series of tragic events pushed Ken to become much more religious. Several relatives, friends, and acquaintances died in accidents, and two grandparents passed away, all in the space of about a year and a half. "Death was becoming a reality" and as a consequence Ken started wondering "What is there after death? Where does God fit in?"

Shortly after these deaths, there was a Billy Graham crusade in the city, and a cousin "went forward to the altar." However, Ken's sister, who also attended the crusade, "thought it was crazy." The cousin became very religious, and Ken accepted his invitation to join a Christian group for boys. The cousin subsequently spoke to the group about life after death. "Because of being a Christian he did not fear death . . . he talked for about twenty minutes about it. Then two weeks later he was killed in a car accident." After the funeral service for his cousin, Ken talked to another cousin who had become a pastor, "and he talked about giving yourself to Christ . . . he really went through the Bible with me."

Shortly thereafter, Ken was home looking after his brother while his parents went out. As he read a special newspaper section on accidents, "it hit me that 75 percent of those killed in the accidents were under twenty-five," but Ken did not "have those assurances" that his Christian cousin had about death: "I did not know where I was going or what would happen after death. So then I prayed, but was quite disappointed because there weren't pink elephants running around the room and a hallelujah chorus . . . I wasn't quite sure what had happened."

In the next year, after another relative's death, Ken inexplicably asked a friend to help him pray for his father. Later he learned that his father had been in a car accident at the time he prayed for him, and was lucky to have survived. Ken's interpretation of these events was that divine intervention was involved: "I really felt that God was in the midst of all this and had really saved my dad, and kind of stopped the chain of events." At this point Ken joined a church, and has remained a committed Christian for twenty-one years. About the same time, his mother also became a Christian and the two attended church together. The father did not immediately join this move toward Christianity, but did eventually attend church as well. Through all of this a close friend acted

166

as a sort of "religious mentor" by helping Ken to study the Bible, by discussing religious issues, and so on. Also, even before his parents became involved with a church, they were very tolerant of Ken's emerging religiousness. "We were never put down for what we thought or didn't think."

To this day, Ken's sister has remained "strongly antireligious." So how does he explain the fact that he became a religious person in spite of his nonreligious upbringing? Ken readily agrees that the most powerful influences were the deaths of people close to him, combined with the strong emotional and religious support he received from specific relatives and friends. He made reference to the fact that he was worried about the implications his disbelief might have for him after death. "At the time I couldn't say, yes, there definitely is an after-death, but if there is, I'm on the wrong side. It is kind of like going into an exam. I go in hoping I get an A and would be happy with a B, rather than going in saying, well, I'm going to get a D on this. Like, I knew I failed the test of eternal life."

Ken is now a very religious person, scoring a "perfect" 216 on the Christian Orthodoxy scale, attending church weekly, getting involved in Bible study groups, praying on an "ongoing" basis, and volunteering through his church. He has no regrets about becoming a Christian, only "I wish it had happened sooner." There have been clear benefits, from his perspective: "I've learned to love myself, accept myself. I have a peace now that is hard to explain. I have an assurance of the future."

The thirteen-year-old Ken would be surprised at the religious changes which took place subsequently, as revealed in our "Back to the Future" scenario. He would simply have trouble grasping the extent of the turn toward religion, even though he was himself somewhat positive about religion at the time.

Now that he has become very religious, Ken feels there is

no turning back. He could not even consider going back to his nonreligious life "because I wouldn't be the person I am now" and "I kind of like the road I'm on. . . . I have the security which I would lose if I went back."

What kind of advice would Ken give to an eighteen-year-old young man who was thinking about becoming more religious? "I would tell him to come on a weekly basis and we'll look at the book of John." There was no thought of exploring the "other" side of the issues. "I believe that God, through his word, is where the power is. . . . I would share my testimony, what God has done for me, and what he can do for him, too." He would also try to become the younger man's friend because having a friend to depend on is "very important when one is going through something."

LAURA

At the highly ordinary age of eighteen for a university freshman, Laura was another Amazing Believer who scored a nearly perfect 215 on the Christian Orthodoxy scale. She and her two younger brothers had never been to church in the large city where they grew up. Her father had been forced to go to Mennonite services as a boy, and he hated it. Her mother had a general interest in religion, but no inclination to "practice it out loud." So Laura's score on the Religious Emphasis Scale came in at a mere 8 out of 96.

When she was seven, Laura's parents let her go to a summer Bible camp with a cousin. The camp "did not focus on a specific religion. It's more just a Christian outlook. I really enjoyed it because of all the activities. I didn't really focus upon the religion too much yet." She has attended the camp almost every year since, now serving as a counselor. "I just loved it. You meet so many people and have so many experiences." The camp is "not really religion based. You have prayers before meals, and you have a devotional. You have Bible studies. I don't know if it's converting, but they do introduce everybody to Christianity. But they don't lay out the Ten Commandments. If you have questions, they have someone to answer them." But the camp focuses more upon activities than praying: "It's like a great party."

Laura remembers believing in God at age nine because of the Bible camp. "I was so scared to do it. You don't really understand it when you're so young." A counselor helped her come to terms with her feelings.

Laura did not go to her parents about this. "We're not really an affectionate family. We don't talk about anything, really." Instead, she interacted a lot with peers at camp and youth groups. Besides singing, these groups invited her and others to share memories, ask for prayers from others, and discuss family problems. She still corresponds regularly with people she met at camp. "Once you leave there, you have hardly anyone around you, and you start slipping."

She has seen others "slip." "There's this guy I know. He went to C.I.T. [Counselors in Training] with me, and for the past couple of years he's been a counselor. He's just great at camp, just a 'perfect little angel' type thing. And then once you get him away, into the school year, he just parties it up and everything, and I can't believe it was him. It could be deceiving the way some people act at camp."

Although Laura has considered herself a Christian since she was nine, she has no denominational allegiance. She does not think of herself as "born again." She still has never been to church in her entire life, believing that being a Christian means asking Jesus into your heart, being saved, and believing that you are saved. She studies the Bible once or twice a month, and prays every night before she goes to bed, usually for better grades and comfort. Overall, Laura earned average grades in school, but with D's in science and math.

Laura's parents know about her beliefs. "They don't disagree with it, and they might even be happy. They just don't display any emotion about it." Laura even suspects her mother and father agreed to her going to the Bible camp because they *wanted* her to become a Christian. But they wanted *her* to choose it, not have it forced upon her as happened to her father.

Laura occasionally second-guesses her choice. "You always wonder, who is this person I'm praying to, God or whatever? Is it the right thing? Is somebody even listening to me, or am I just doing this to help me along, get my thoughts organized type of thing?" But she thinks it unlikely she would ever drop Christianity. "I believe that I'm going to heaven."

Her "Back to the Future" adventure would prove fairly uneventful: "I knew at seven what Christianity was about. She'd be happy for me."

Laura has long had a "strictness problem" with her parents. "I'm eighteen, and this past Saturday I had to be back in the house by midnight," she said with visible anger. Laura's parents wouldn't let her have a boyfriend, or go to night dances when she was thirteen. "I would sit in my room and just sulk. It was so bad. I didn't see what was wrong with it. Everybody else was going." Her mother and father still don't like her going out. But "I have never talked back to my parents," obeying strictly all her life. Her parents threatened to kick her out of the house if she was late. Laura thinks her parents' strictness comes from their own bad experiences when young. "They don't want me to make the same mistakes they did. But it's time for them to let go."

Laura felt she had given up nothing by becoming a Christian. "I don't smoke or do drugs as it is. I have a social drink now and then. I don't think I've given up any fun stuff." When asked what she had gotten out of her transition, she replied, "I've gotten a sense of answers to questions like 'Where did everything come from?' I've made a lot of new friends, people to talk to about these questions. And also a sense of organization. You know what you can do, and what you cannot. You can give food to the homeless, but some people can't be helped."

Asked why she would not someday give up her beliefs, Laura said, "The sins that you'd commit, the things that you did wrong, would not be forgiven. You would have to live with that guilt. Eternal life is always a big question. Do you really die, or does your soul live on?"

If a young girl with no religious background began to wonder about things, and approached Laura for advice about becoming more religious, Laura would "make sure she knows the facts. Tell her how she can become a Christian if she wants to. Make sure she knows that Jesus died for our sins. Make sure she wants this, because you don't want to force her. If she wants to do it, she can go ahead on her own and do it. I wouldn't force her, though."

Laura was unsure how she would raise her children, although she would give them more opportunity to go to church than she had. "I'd be more open about it. We don't talk about God, we don't talk about death and what happens. We don't talk about anything." And she definitely would send her children to Bible camp.

MEL

Mel, at twenty-seven, had put more years behind him than most of our other interviewees. The firstborn of two children, he grew up on a farm just outside a small city. His father had been raised in the United Church, and his mother came from a Catholic background. Neither practiced either, however, and they did not talk about religion to their children. Mel had been to a United Church Sunday School several times during his youth, and to Mass twice. His score of 10 on the Religious Emphasis Scale says it all.

As Mel's farm lay near a "very religious town," most of his schoolmates were Christians. He felt a little left out, but also became angry when they "pushed their attitudes onto me."

After he graduated from high school, where he described his grades as "very low," Mel moved to the nearby city where he got a job as a mechanic. He developed a heavy drinking habit during these years. "At nineteen I was into parties, fast cars, hot women, and cold beer." But several traffic violations squelched Mel's dream of becoming a police officer, he said. He also had become "a bit violent" several times when drunk.

One day when he was twenty-one, Mel wandered into the "low part of town." He found himself wondering how the residents had ended up there. He also realized that he might end up there, too, if he did not take control of his life. He set to work curbing his drinking. Among other things, he started hanging out at a coffee shop in the city rather than the bars.

A waitress at this coffee shop caught his eye. She invited Mel and other patrons to a "party-type thing" one night at her church. "We were told they were going to show some

172

films, and different activities were planned. No pressure, nothing put on you. So a group of us went. They showed a film, and it made us think a bit. The people I met there that one day showed interest in me, more than people normally do. There was just something different about them. They were very open around each other." Mel started attending the (Mennonite) church.

Mel's parents were separating at the time, and he was living away from home. But he was always close to them, and "they really watched me" as he became more religious. They knew he was pursuing the waitress at the time, and so wondered if he was just "chasing the girl." After a while, they saw it was more than that. "My dad isn't open to religion at all. He listens, but he doesn't accept." But his mother brings up religion once in a while. When Mel unexpectedly lost his job, his mother told him, "It's all right. I had a feeling from God that everything would be fine."

Asked if his mother had accepted Jesus as her personal savior, Mel answered "She would say 'Yes.' But—I really hate being judgmental—when it came down to the actual 'This is what you then have to do,' she couldn't do it."

As Mel attended church, he made many friends: "I have fifty, sixty people in the church who are my friends, and only two or three outside." He started attending a College and Career Group for young adults at the church, but mostly "I searched by myself." Two years after that first visit, at age twenty-three, Mel was baptized in the Mennonite church. "That was the farthest thing from my mind that I thought I would do." He and the waitress were married the following year. "But I made it a point to prove to myself that I wanted to become a Christian for itself, not for her."

Mel now goes to church at least once a week. "I try to read

my Bible every day. We pray before every meal," although they do it discreetly when they sense it would upset others. He and his wife regularly participate in a Bible study group. Mel has never felt any guilt or fear over becoming religious. He pegs the chances of his becoming nonreligious again at "zero."

If his present self journeyed back in time and revealed the future to the nineteen-year-old Mel, he would be told to "F— off! Get out of my way." How would the older Mel explain the change, then? "Something just started to click into place. There has to be more to life than drinking and running around. To me, the world was just getting worse and worse. The more you looked at things, the more sense religion made. When I was twenty, a friend showed me a Christian magazine, and told me it had dramatically changed his life. It sort of made me think, 'What am I going to be like in the future?'"

When asked what had enabled him to become the only religious person in his family, Mel answered, "I don't think there's anything different, other than I just started to think about myself and my future, what was my life going to be like if I didn't stop drinking."

Becoming religious has cost Mel several friends, who mock him now. So he does not associate with them. And discussions with his family can "get strained." On the other hand, Mel listed many gains from his decision. "I have more confidence in myself, and a better sense of who I am. I'm able to talk to people a lot easier now. And I have a pretty good weapon if somebody wants to come up and preach to me. If they push their view on me, I'll push my view on them. That generally turns them off."

Not surprisingly, Mel feels no temptation to return to his former ways: "Looking back at it now, I didn't really enjoy my life back then. I was less healthy. My attitude toward other people was very self-centered. Things like speeding, flying down the street with no cares." He and his wife intend to give their children a different upbringing than he had, when it comes to religion, rearing them as strong Mennonites.

Asked what he would say to a young searcher wondering about Christianity, Mel said, "I'm not one to push religion at all. I get turned off by people who do that. I'd tell him what I went through. I'd explain my religious beliefs. But I'd always allow him to say, 'I don't want to talk about that.' And that's fine. Not every successful person, or happy person, is a religious person."

NORA

Nora, nineteen, has one older sister. Her parents were divorced when she was very young, and she lived with her atheistic father until she was eleven, then moved in with her mother, who became a "weak" Christian shortly thereafter. Her mother "didn't put any pressure on us, just told us a little about what she was discovering with her religion." When Nora was about fifteen, she moved back with her father and his wife, which is when she started to think about religion more and to read the Bible.

She never attended church when she was growing up, except for a single occasion when a grandparent took her to a Catholic church one Christmas. Until Nora was eleven, there was absolutely no other contact with any religious group or activity that she can remember, which helps to explain her Religious Emphasis score of just 10.

So why did Nora start to become more religious? One might suspect that in the years she lived with her mother, the mother's Christianity might have influenced Nora to become more religious herself, but Nora herself does not think so. "When my mom started talking about it, I listened but I was kind of skeptical because my dad was so against it. It wasn't really until I was about fourteen or fifteen that I started looking into it myself." Nora's explanation for her initial turn to religion is different. "It might have been more personal. Maybe I was looking for something. I was going through a lot of stuff with my parents and maybe I was searching for something and that was an ideal answer. I don't really know." There was no specific event, or religious teaching, that seemed to trigger her turn to religion.

There were other "problems with parents" in Nora's life at this time, most notably with her stepmother. This latter conflict prompted her to move and live at her mother's house. This took some adjustment, "getting to know my mom again, after not living with her for a long time . . . I was looking for more security or something." However, when her mother moved to another community, Nora decided to move back in with her father so she could live in the area she was familiar with. None of the conflict involved religion.

She did not experience any guilt or fear when she began to become more religious. She did take some of her questions about religion to her mother, "who was more than happy to answer them. But I also felt like I didn't really want to believe just what she believed. I wanted to find out for myself." Nora also talked with her father, who explained that he didn't believe in God: "If that's what you believe, fine, but it's not for me." She also talked with her older sister, "who started to look into it about the same time as I did." In fact, both Nora

176

and her sister have boyfriends who belong to a fundamentalist church, "so I've been looking into [their denomination] a bit more." She does occasionally go to church now when visiting her mother, but can't remember what denomination it is.

Nora feels no fear or guilt now about her religious beliefs and in fact "feels better." She also thinks it is very unlikely that she would ever go back to her nonreligious views. How would her younger self react to the now religious Nora? With shock and disbelief: "You're crazy. I can't believe it." She would try to explain the surprising change in herself by saying, "I feel more secure. I feel an actual sense of comfort from knowing that I believe and it makes me feel so much better. I feel so much better about my faith and where I'm going in my life and what is going to happen when I die, than when I was younger." She commented that the young Nora would not be satisfied with this explanation because "I didn't really think about my future and death that much when I was younger."

When asked to explain why she became more religious, in spite of the fact that the majority of people in her situation remain nonreligious, Nora replied that she couldn't understand why other people didn't read and learn more about religion. They, too, would become more religious if they only knew more about it, "instead of just ignoring it altogether."

Nora does feel that there has been some "cost" to her becoming religious, especially her inclination to "feel guilty if I'm not living the proper Christian life, like if I don't go to church, or if I do something like go out drinking." In addition, "I feel badly for my dad because he won't accept it at all." She also finds that there has been some cost in terms of her relationship with her boyfriend because his religion is so different from hers. On the other hand, there are benefits such as, "I feel more secure. I'm just happy to have faith instead of just living and thinking, well, I'm going to die some day. I have the knowledge that when I die I'm going to be with my family and my friends. Also, I look to God for guidance and I just feel better." Nora admits that it might be easier to return to her nonreligious life "given all the conflict and stuff," but she couldn't do it "because of what I know now . . . I would feel too guilty."

If a fourteen-year-old with a history similar to her own came to Nora for advice about religion, she would "just say don't really listen to what anyone else says. Just look into it for yourself and go to the library, read the Bible, go to different churches. . . . I would say look into all of them and find which one's right for you."

ORSON

Orson, eighteen, now goes to a fundamentalist church every week, more often when a Bible study group meets in midweek. He reads the Bible every night, prays daily, and has helped out with Sunday School and youth group. But before grade 10, Orson's life was very different.

He comes from a family of six children who grew up in a northern community. His mother was Roman Catholic and father Protestant, but "my parents never went to church." His sisters did go to church occasionally, however, and so did Orson. His older brother had been an altar boy and convinced Orson to try it for a couple of years as well. But he was "not very serious" about it, going "just when I felt like it." He did attend a Catholic elementary school, but when his parents gave him the choice of which high school to go to, he chose the public one.

When he was still in elementary school, Orson "started getting into the rough crowd." He hung around with fellows who had no interest in religion at all. They swore a lot, and he would "look for other pleasures in life through alcohol and parties and stuff." "We were the popular people, like the basketball team in grades 7 and 8." While Orson is careful to point out that this crowd was not "criminal" and he never did drugs he readily admits he is not happy with his attitudes and behavior at this time of his life. He argued with his parents about his girlfriend: "It was kind of an immature relationship, so I was very hard to get along with." This rather turbulent early adolescence left Orson feeling empty. When he was about fifteen, he began to think about his life's direction. "In the end, when I analyzed it all, it didn't make me happy. So I started thinking that there must be something more to life."

Orson remembers having had vague thoughts when he was in elementary school about things like "does God really exist," but "I just forgot about it after that." Then, in grade 10, he and his best friend started going to a church youth group. Orson's friend was initially "going out for the girls," but within a year became seriously religious. However, his friend's turn to religion made Orson all the more determined that he would never let religion enter his life in the same way: "I guess I was kind of scared or guilty. I didn't know what my friends or family would think, and I always tried to be in the 'in crowd,' you know." But it was not long before he followed in his friend's footsteps.

The importance of peers in this "conversion" experience cannot be overemphasized. Orson is very clear that his current religiousness "was not influenced by my parents, it was

179

influenced by my friends." He never talked to anyone else about his religious questions and concerns, except his friends. Orson was impressed with the fact that his religious friends "always had answers," and before long, he found himself agreeing with their religious views.

After he was converted, Orson shared his new religious views with his parents, who until that time were in the dark about the changes in their son. His parents "didn't really have any" reaction to the news. Orson has since shared his religious views with other relatives and friends and feels their reaction has typically been "if that's what you think is best, it is okay with me."

Any guilt or fear associated with his turn to religion has dissipated, especially since "I think everybody knows now." Nor can Orson see any possibility of his returning to his previous views and lifestyle. He remembers how unsatisfying his life was before he became a born-again Christian—the alcohol, the emphasis on material goods, the partying, and "the next morning not feeling so hot. I don't want to have a reputation of that kind of person when I grow up. I don't want to be like that."

If, when he was about thirteen, Orson had been told he would turn out to be this religious, he simply would not have believed it. How could he explain the changes which would have shocked his younger self? "Look, I was into all kinds of pleasures but I didn't find what I wanted there." He would then explain what he has learned from the Bible.

Why did Orson turn to religion when others like him do not? In addition to the important influence of his friends, he mused, "Once you get older you have to start thinking about the future, about what happens after death, and so on. You don't have to be really old to die. I've had friends of my

friends die. I haven't known these people but they died at a
very young age. Just freak accidents."

Orson feels that his religiousness has cost him something
in his friendships, since some of his friends have made it clear
that they do not approve of his turn to religion: "I wish some
of my friends would be more accepting of me." When they express their disapproval, Orson's reaction is to "talk to them
about the Bible and how Christ came and died for everyone,
not just for me." He also describes his personal search for
meaning in life.

There are benefits to being religious in his view, especially
since "the Bible says that if we live a life for God, for Christ,
we will be much more rewarded in heaven after we die. If you
have accepted Christ as your personal savior you will get to
heaven, it is guaranteed. Even if I turn back, God will still
take me in, but he'll have to be just with me."

Orson's advice to a confused fourteen-year-old would
involve explaining "what the Bible says that Christ has done
for us and that no matter what we do, he'll always accept us.
He'll always love us and there is always a place for us in
heaven. And that when we get to heaven, we will be ultimately
satisfied."

A little more than a year before the interview, Orson's
father died. "It brought a lot of questions to my mind and I
think it kind of made me wobble a bit on where I stand in my
faith. It was the hardest time because questions that I may
have asked myself would be like, why would somebody like
my father have to die at a young age? Whereas other people
have fathers who beat them or who beat their wives and they
are still alive. I would ask God these questions, in the end
knowing that he has reasons for everything and that I can't
try and figure him out. I don't think I would want to have a

faith in a God that I understood 100 percent. But it's helped me to grow stronger, I think, and to come closer to him and to rely more on him."

PAM

The firstborn of two children raised in a medium-sized city, Pam at age twenty presented one of the most dramatic of all our Amazing Believer cases. Her score on the Religious Emphasis scale had been a barely ticking three. Yet she chalked up a perfect 216/216 on the Christian Orthodoxy scale.

Neither of Pam's parents had been very religious. Her mother came from a strong Catholic family, but, for reasons Pam did not know, had never practiced the religion as an adult. Her father had no faith. Not surprisingly then, her parents did not talk about religion with Pam as she was growing up: "We never did talk much at all, actually. We were not the closest family." Her parents separated when she was ten. But her mother had to work, and Pam was home alone "almost all my life," especially after her mother fell in love again.

Her religious awakening began just one year ago, when her father died after a serious illness: "I knew I needed more in my life. I wanted to go to heaven." The interviewer asked where this belief in heaven had come from. "I knew there was a right and wrong," Pam replied. "I knew there was a heaven and hell. But I didn't know anything about God, or the Bible at all." She worried about where her father had gone after death.

At this point in her life, Pam's best friend took her to a religious conference produced by a traveling evangelist. She promised it would change Pam's life and tell her how to solve her problems. Pam did not know the "seminar" was religious when she agreed to go as her friend's guest. Once there, she was introduced to various people. "There was this woman there who was very understanding, very kind. She told me to come to church with my friend. So I went with her a couple of times, and I wasn't too sure on it yet. It's a pretty neat church, so I liked it. This woman knew that I had problems, knew that I was really upset. So she gave me some Bible teachings, and invited me to her home. She's been a big part of my life, very inspirational."

This particular church was set up for young adults by a Mennonite group. "But they don't really teach Mennonite values. Just scripture and things." The service is nontraditional: "A band plays for about fifteen minutes. Then there is a play on what the lecture is going to be about. Then the minister talks."

As often proved the case in previous histories, Pam's mother has been happy for her daughter's spiritual awakening. "But she's a little bitter toward this woman now, probably because I find her so fascinating, and I don't hold the same feelings toward her [i.e., Pam's mother]. Whenever I talk about it, she kind of moves away." Asked what other things might have led her to become a believer, Pam said, "When I was growing up, I didn't really have a care in the world. I drank, etcetera, I was a 'party girl.' And I felt something was missing. There wasn't anything to live for. And I needed more in my life."

Pam has never felt guilty or afraid about the dramatic change in her life. Everyone knows about her transition. She has several good friends from high school with whom she used to go out, who are happy for her conversion because it has made Pam so happy.

She described herself as "a Christian," but not a member of any denomination. She was about to be baptized in just a few weeks, and goes to church every Sunday. She reads the Bible every night. She also prays then, and during the day "if things are going badly." Typically she asks for forgiveness, and prays for other people in her life. She prays that her mother will become a Christian. Pam thinks it very unlikely that she herself would ever go back to her old ways.

How would the eighteen-year-old Pam react to what has happened? "She'd probably laugh and say 'You're crazy. I don't believe it.'" Why? "Because at that time, I wasn't at all doing Christian practices. I was totally the opposite, drinking and swearing and having sex. I never thought in a million years I would be what I am now." How would the "now Pam" explain this change to the "then Pam"? "Probably the death of my father," she replied.

Pam said her grades in high school had been "pretty high, averaging about a B+."

The interviewer then explained how unusual it was for someone with no religious background to become so devout. "So what's different about you?" Pam answered, "I don't know. I'm pretty accepting of things. I don't push them away because they're stupid. I think things through. If they make sense to me, I'll accept them. Like the Bible. Most people think it's just a bunch of stories. But they deal with life. They can help you with whatever is wrong."

Pam's only regret about her turn to religion is that she didn't turn sooner. "I'm a lot stronger now. I was very weak before. My self-confidence [was] down. Now I have more self-discipline. I'm a lot happier, for sure." She does, however, have a problem now with her boyfriend of the past three years: "He's still a non-Christian. He's very supportive, and happy for me. But he says it's not for him. It's been hard. I've prayed to help me through this. I'm still debating whether to still see him."

When asked why she would not go back to her old ways, Pam replied, "They were pointless. They didn't make me happy." She regrets her former life, but is not ashamed: "We all make mistakes."

If a peer with a nonreligious background sought her advice on whether to become a Christian, Pam said, "I probably wouldn't tell her my beliefs. I wouldn't push them on her. I'm new to these things, I probably don't know as much as others do. I'd probably tell her to talk to someone at my church. There are counselors there. I'd also tell her how it changed me, made me a better person."

Pam intends to tell her children about her life. Also, "I'd teach them things out of the Bible, what is right and wrong. I'd take them to church. Then I'd let them decide when they're older. I wouldn't push it on them if they didn't want it."

THE OTHER AMAZING BELIEVERS

Some of the other Amazing Believers we interviewed, you will see, had histories similar to the ones detailed above. We also found a number of students who looked like Amazing Believers *on paper*, but whose "+4's" turned out to be mainly due to their "cultural heritage" in a Christian society, not something having *personal* meaning. In other cases the beliefs appear to have arisen for nonreligious reasons, and proved unconnected to the students' lives.

185

Quinella became an orthodox "believer" in a somewhat unorthodox way. At twelve, she saw a religious poster printed in green, her "lucky color." She began reading the Bible for exactly thirty minutes each day amidst other "rituals." She was later diagnosed as suffering from an obsessive-compulsive disorder. She has never thought of herself as a Christian, and has never gone to church.

Roger's commitment to Christianity also did not match his answers to our survey. He scored highly on the Christian Orthodoxy scale because he attended Sunday School when young and was taught "this is what you're supposed to believe." But he never prays. Nor does he go to church, because he plays hockey on Sundays. "I can build more friendships playing hockey than in a church."

Samantha also scored higher in beliefs than in behavior. Practicing for gymnastics keeps her from attending church. She prays before competitions, "when it's dark outside," and when she thinks about death. She has only read scripture once, and feels baptism is irrelevant. Samantha could name only one of the Ten Commandments, and knew only the story of Adam and Eve from the Bible.

Todd had many Baptist relatives who taught him Christian beliefs, but his parents gave him no religious training. He says he is a "Pentecostal," but does not know what they believe. He does not go to church, and could find no way his religious beliefs affected his life beyond "saying a little prayer at night." Todd admitted, "Maybe I don't know as much about my religion as I should."

Ulla scored a perfect 216 on the Christian Orthodoxy scale, and meant every word of it. Her awakening began through a romantic involvement with a firmly believing Christian. She prays and reads the Bible often, but rejects organized religions. Ulla's beliefs have enabled her to control a bad temper, and have given her a sense of peace and security in God's love.

Victor was sent to a Catholic school by apostate parents for academic reasons. His religion teachers "really hit home." He found Christianity "made total sense," and Jesus' teachings resonated with his "compassionate nature." Victor goes to Mass about once a month and prays each night. But he rejects baptism, could not "get into" the Bible, and "hasn't the time for a commitment now."

Wendy went to Sunday school until age ten, when her parents divorced. Religion then ceased to be a factor in her life. She has a troubled past, and ran away from home at fourteen. She married and had a child, but then walked away from an abusive husband. When she received a gift of a picture with three Bible verses, it convinced her to become a religious person. Wendy has "back-slid many times from Christianity, but God still loves me, he's understanding and forgiving." Religion has become the "rock of salvation" in her life.

Xavier's turbulent childhood involved the murder of a close relative and a split family. After a "period of atheism" in his mid-teens, he became more religious because "I was always taught to believe that spirits were angels. . . . If I had to believe in spirits, I had to believe in angels, and God made angels, so I had to start believing in God again." He continues to lead a troubled life, not talking with his stepmother, "fighting" with his father, and seeing a psychiatrist for personal difficulties. Xavier's religion is "personal" and he never attends church.

5

An Analysis of the Amazing Believer Cases

What have you noticed in the cases of the Amazing Believers? Who are they? What are their backgrounds, and why do you think they became believers? Which religion did they join, and what did they get out of it? Again, we shall look at the scores the ABs posted on our survey instruments. But mainly we shall study the interviews to trace the journey these twenty-four persons took from nonreligious upbringings to a strong acceptance of Christian teachings.

SURVEY SCORES

We noted in the case descriptions that the Amazing Believers' Religious Emphasis scores ranged from the rock bottom 0 (Cam) to a still very low 11 (Quinella, Victor, and Ulla).

Overall they averaged 6.9 on this sixteen-item scale, which works out to 0.43 per item—or practically zero. So none of these interviewees had been steeped in religion, and most had not even gotten close to the teapot. Ten said they had never been to church as children, and ten others had just gone "once in a while" at Christmas and the like.

Yet these students very strongly accepted the basic tenets of Christianity. Their Christian Orthodoxy scores topped the scale, ranging from a very high 189 to the maximum 216, and averaging 205.9. Six of them scored a "perfect" 216, and three others just missed with 215s. Thus the Amazing Believers greatly believed, *much* more so than typical students at our universities.

Right-Wing Authoritarianism (RWA) scores (indicating the "follower" authoritarian personality, and described in chapter 3) went from a very low 72 to a very high 224, averaging 141.7—higher than the total sample average of 123.8. Half of the Amazing Believers were "High RWAs," landing in the top quartile of the RWA distribution, while only five were "Lows."

The Amazing Believers recruited in 1995 also answered our Religious Questions and Religious Doubts scales. Rather surprisingly, given their backgrounds, questions about religion had arisen as often in their minds as they had in the sample as a whole. Their "Twenty Questions" scores ranged from 31 (Mel) to 99 (Frieda) and averaged 55.9, virtually identical to the 55.1 found overall. However, they ended up with few doubts about religion. Their "Twenty Doubts" scores spread from an astonishing 0 (Ivan and Ulla) to 30 (Victor) and averaged only 20.5, not even half the 42.8 of the overall sample. Given their very high scores on the Christian Orthodoxy scale, these low levels of doubt certainly make sense. Whatever questions had arisen in their minds about religion, they had found very satisfying answers.

VITAL STATISTICS

Gender

Our ABs were twice as likely to be women as men (sixteen to eight). This 67 percent turnout of females slightly exceeds the 58 percent female composition of the screening sample. As such, it fits with the general research finding that women tend to be more religious than men.[1]

Birth Order

Half of the Amazing Believers were firstborn in their families (including four "only children"), nine (37.5 percent) were second-born, and three (12.5 percent) were third or subsequent children. These percentages, virtually identical to those found among the Amazing Apostates, again do not support the stereotype that firstborns are more likely to accept their parents' beliefs. Most of the ABs' families contained just one or two children, but five families had three children and four others had more than that.

Age

As was the case for our AAs, the median age of the ABs equalled nineteen. However, two "greybeards" (Ken and Wendy) had passed thirty.

Home Religion

A few of our ABs (e.g., Ken and Roger) said they had always considered themselves Christians. But most were raised in no faith whatsoever. Ten of our Amazing Believers insisted that they *never* went to church when they were growing up, and another ten said they had gone but rarely.

AMAZING BELIEVERS IN THE INTERVIEWS

Some Amazing Believers Are Not Such Amazing Believers

As was true with the Amazing Apostates, one can reasonably argue that our trawling of the introductory psychology classes with the Religious Emphasis and Christian Orthodoxy scales netted some students who are not "really" Amazing Believers. Roger and Quinella could easily be discarded. Roger said he had simply given what he thought to be the socially "right" answers to the Christian Orthodoxy scale,

191

while Quinella's beliefs arose from her obsessive-compulsive disorder. In both cases, their religion had no discernible connection to their lives.

How much connection should we require then? Nora, Samantha, and Todd seem only slightly more religious than Roger, and Xavier's case resembles Quinella's. Six of the remaining ABs (Art, Gil, Heather, Jill, Laura, and Ulla) belonged to no church and never intended to join one. They had simply developed a personal belief system which included acceptance of basic Christian teachings.

These twelve possible exclusions comprise half of our supply of potential ABs. Yet we have not even considered whether "believers" should go to church regularly. Art said, "You don't have to go to church," and Gil believed it had nothing to do with being a "real Christian." But if you think it does, you will also discard Ed and Victor. Yet some of the ABs themselves required much *more* than that. Cam observed that his sister calls herself a Christian, but "she doesn't really live a Christian life." Mel felt that even though his mother says she has accepted Jesus as her personal savior, she really hasn't. And Ken said, "Just because you go to church, that doesn't make you a Christian." If you hold that someone who deeply believes in Christianity should have an active religious life, going to church regularly and reading scripture and praying, then we only have ten "Amazing *Real* Believers": Bev, Cam, Diane, Frieda, Ivan, Ken, Mel, Orson, Pam, and Wendy.

It is impossible to know scientifically where to redraw the line, so we shall leave it where we drew it originally. We shall keep all the ABs who met our criteria, just as we kept all the AAs. But since some believers had stricter criteria for being Christians than others did, we shall come back to this issue of the "Real Believers" versus the rest at the end of this chapter.

The Conversion Process

We checked to see if the ABs' turn to religion was sometimes sparked by a feeling of being "out of place." After all, they were nonreligious in a Christian culture, did not go to church when their friends did, and so on. But that can be set aside. Only Mel reported feeling he was an "outsider" as a child.

Then when did the conversion begin? It happened at quite different times for different people. Laura began to believe in God when she was seven. Wendy began her journey back to Christianity when she was twenty-six. The average equaled 16.2 years. Once our pilgrims began, they soon considered themselves "Christians" or members of a particular denomination—by age 17.7 on average. In eleven cases, the transformation from nonreligious to believer took a year or less.

When we interviewed the Amazing *Apostates*, we tried to pinpoint the first question that had eventually led to their loss of faith. In return, when talking with the Amazing Believers, we tried to isolate the first belief that eventually led to their conversion. We almost never found one, however. They never said, for example, that a particular Bible *story* was the first thing they believed in. Jill comes closest with her early doubting of science's account of creation.

Instead the converts typically reached a point when they decided to accept all the beliefs at once. They sometimes even went from nonbelievers to strong believers in a flash. As Bev put it, "It all became clear to me at once. I decided that Christianity was the right path to take. I started praying." Cam in turn described it like this: "It just hit home that day. Everything clicked together and it made sense. It was just sort of an awakening." Diane crossed over the bridge the day she did well on her math exam. Ken had his moment of reve-lation as he walked home from a Campus Crusade. Mel said, "Something just started to click into place."

Why Were They Searching?

The Amazing Believers came to religion down several dif-ferent paths. But surely you noticed the most heavily trodden path one as you read the case studies. Over half of the ABs (Art, Bev, Cam, Frieda, Ivan, Jill, Ken, Mel, Nora, Orson, Pam, Quinella, Wendy, and Xavier) had serious personal problems at the time they began to convert. Alcohol was the most common denominator. But others had intense psycho-logical difficulties, ranging from Art, whose depression and uncertainty about the future at age fourteen kept him in his room worrying, to Jill, whose very alienating, isolating, lonely life at fourteen made her angry and spiteful, to Cam, who said he had "every single kind of problem that you could even think of." Many ABs needed an anchor to stabilize their lives. Others felt, after finding life in the "fast lane" unsatis-fying, that there had to be more meaning to existence, that something was missing.

Experiences with death seemed to be especially powerful influences for six of the ABs. Ken was confronted the most, as six people in his life had died in rapid succession when he was a teenager. He couldn't help but wonder "What is there after death? Where does God fit in?" Xavier's mother was murdered when he was seven. (It was seeing her ghost subsequently that strengthened his beliefs in spirits and angels, beliefs that even-tually led to accepting his Christianity.) Diane was still so traumatized by the deaths in her family that she began to cry when the subject of death came up in the interview.

Insight?

If you want a one-word explanation of what started the fifteen ABs just mentioned down the road to religion, we would say it was fear. It struck from several directions: fear of what would happen to them if they did not overcome their problems, fear of death itself, fear of what might happen to them after they died. If you want a second-place cause, it would be loneliness, often accompanied by the depressing feeling that their life was empty.

One cannot find such connecting threads in the nine remaining AB cases. Ed did not have any particular problems in life; he was instead attracted by the happiness Christians seemed to enjoy. Gil found religion filled a void in his life he actually had not felt before. Heather wondered "Why am I here?" and almost casually decided to believe in God because it made everything simpler. Laura converted at such an early age (nine), it is hard to determine her reason; she herself did not know. Samantha is only religious when she is afraid, and Roger and Todd are not religious even then. Ulla feels she has always believed, and just needed her boyfriend to rekindle her faith. Victor accepted Christianity because it fit in with his compassionate nature.

Insight?

What do the nine "hard to categorize" people above have in common? They are all generic Christians, and basically inactive. None of them belongs to any denomination, none but Ed has been baptized, and they almost never go to church. To put it another way, when the conversion did not meet strong emotional needs, it never led to dedication.

How Did They Become Religious?

If the Amazing Believers usually turned to religion because of personal problems or fear of death, they were almost always led to Christianity by their *peers*. Often their friends began by taking them on a religiously sponsored recreational outing to go skiing, to play volleyball, to sing songs, or to go to a "party-type thing." In a few instances (Bev, Gil, Mel, and Ulla), the future AB was romantically interested in the "friend." But usually (Art, Cam, Ed, Frieda, Ivan, Jill, Ken, Orson, and Pam) a best friend or a group of good friends showed the way. The ABs then found the Youth Group, the Christian Fellowship, the "people at the church," or the friends they made at Bible Camp very accepting and supportive as they worked out their problems. As Mel put it, "The people I met there that one day showed interest in me, more than people normally do." And when Cam was not sure, for the first few months after his conversion, that he had done the right thing, "that's really when my Christian friends rallied around me and made sure that I was comfortable. They were very, very supportive. It was really nice. . . . Through them I have found a lot of the nurturing that I don't get at home." Bev put it similarly, "They loved me more than my own family did."

We should also note the several instances in which students became more religious after they thought God had answered their prayers. Diane received help with her exams, and later got a new boyfriend. Ed's girlfriend returned early from a canoe trip. Ivan believed God gave him his fiancée as a reward for stopping drinking. Ken felt his prayers saved his father's life in the automobile accident.

Guilt and Fear

Only three of these students (Cam, Heather, and Orson) admitted to *any* guilt or fear about becoming religious, and even these concerns were relatively minor (e.g., "I wondered if I was doing the right thing at the time"). In almost all of the twenty-four cases, while they seldom brought their growing beliefs to their parents before they had made their final decision, they felt their mothers and fathers would understand. And they were right; most of the parents responded either neutrally (nine) or positively (eleven). (Even if you are an atheist, your teenage children can do many things worse than become religious.) Heather and Ulla come closest to being "closet Christians," keeping their beliefs quite private.

Present Religion

Which denominations attracted the Amazing Believers? Most (fourteen) said they were "Christian" or "no religion." For those who did indicate an affiliation, nearly all chose fundamentalist Protestant denominations (Baptist, Mennonite, Pentecostal, Alliance, or a local Bible Chapel). Just one was Catholic and one Anglican. Two more who simply said they were "Christian" allowed that they attended a Baptist church. Thus our Amazing Believers had little inclination to join any organized religion. Those who did usually took a pass on mainstream Catholic or Protestant churches, and chose the conservative churches that had reached out to them.

"Back to the Future"

If they were able to travel back in time and tell their younger selves about the tremendous change soon to occur in their lives, most of our ABs thought their former selves would be struck with disbelief. Four said they would be "surprised," and twelve went further, namely, that they would be shocked or amazed when told about becoming religious. Just five ABs thought their younger selves would understand. (Three did not answer the question.)

How would they explain the "about turn" in their religious beliefs? Bev would say, "When you go through all the negatives, and finally you find some positive in your life, you feel a love that you never felt before." Cam would explain, "You are going to be going through some pretty deep, heavy stuff. But you are going . . . to take charge of your life." Frieda would point out "if you don't have God, it's pretty lonely." Heather would observe, "I needed . . . something stable in my life." Ivan would reveal, "Bible camps were an 'up' and partying brought me down." Jill would recall all her "anger, confusion, naivete, and ignorance." Orson would talk about all the "downers." "I was into all kinds of pleasures but I didn't find what I wanted there." Pam would simply say to her younger self, "Dad dies."

198

Insight?

As was the case for the Amazing Apostates, most of the Amazing Believers' responses in the "Back to the Future" scenario dramatized the enormous change that had taken place in their lives. If anything, they disassociated themselves even more from their earlier selves, for they had much to regret. Nothing could be clearer to them than the night-and-day difference in their happiness now. They had been "born again."

Did Problems with Parents Help Cause the Conversion?

If some people might become apostates as a way of rebelling against very religious parents, then, arguably, others might become religious as a way of rebelling against atheistic parents. But that never seemed to be the case in these stories. The parents proved very tolerant and seldom opposed their children's conversion.

Nevertheless, many of the ABs came from troubled families. Five (Cam, Jill, Mel, Nora, and Wendy) had divorced parents, and Xavier had lost his mother at a tender age. Bev, Gil, Laura, and Pam all commented that their families were not close, that people did not talk much to each other. Nora, Orson and Ulla all had considerable conflict with their parents during their teenage years.

Insight?

If the Amazing Believers did not become religious in rebellion against their parents, their unhappy backgrounds still help

199

explain the trouble they often got into during their lives, and the resulting feelings of fear, loneliness, and depression. Thus the ABs do not challenge our theories of socialization as much as we initially supposed. Instead we can see that their family backgrounds indirectly helped shape the dramatic changes that occurred.

Grades

The ABs had somewhat more mixed grades in high school than did the AAs. Seven reported being exceptional or receiving straight A's, and nine others reported a mix of A's and B's. But five reported being "average" or "C" students, and two reported earning below average grades (mostly D's).[2]

Costs and Benefits

Our ABs were hard pressed to find ways in which they had suffered from their turn to religion. Bev, Diane, Ed, Gil, Mel, and Orson all said they had lost friends; but that was a price they gladly paid. They sometimes initiated the separation, in fact. Nora observed that she now gets to feeling guilty for "not living the proper Christian life." But most of them could not think of any costs at all.

As for benefits, as Cam put it, "Do you have another tape?" But the first thing Cam mentioned, *security*, was named more often than anything else by the ABs. This security often sprang from knowing God would make things turn

200

out all right, as Art put it. Heather used nearly the same words: "there's someone out there watching over me and everything will be okay." Ken said, "I have a peace now that is hard to explain. I have an assurance of the future . . . I have the security which I would lose if I went back." Ulla knew "God will help me and protect me. I have nothing to worry about." Ed said something quite similar: "God is always there, and he watches over everyone." Gil put it this way: "It gives me someone to tell my problems to." God was always on the other end of the line, listening.

Nora's security, like others', extended to *heaven*: "Instead of just living and thinking, 'Well, I'm going to die some day,' I have the knowledge that when I die I'm going to be with my family and friends." Heather said, "I don't want to think I'm here and then I'm dead and I'm gone." Laura echoed this: "I believe that I'm going to heaven." Frieda stated, "I definitely believe there's a heaven and I believe the only way to get there is by the death that Jesus died on the cross." Pam said that after her father died, "I knew I needed more in my life. I wanted to go to heaven." Xavier listed heaven as the main benefit: "You're not just gonna die and pass into oblivion." Orson even felt that once he accepted Jesus as his personal savior, he was guaranteed a place in heaven, even if he turned back to his former ways.

Happiness was also mentioned often. Bev spoke for many when she said, "I'm extremely happy right now, a lot happier than I have ever been." Diane had been given a new life: "I really feel reborn." Ed responded, "I was happy before, but it has made me lots happier." Frieda felt her heart, which was "very empty" during her drinking days, was not at all empty now. Pam, who had similar "partying days," said, "I'm a lot happier, for sure."

201

Other benefits were also mentioned often. Bev, Ivan, Jill, Mel, and Ulla all felt they could not control alcohol abuse or emotional problems without their faith. Most of them, plus Diane and Ed, had also found a romantic love through religion. Many mentioned the new friends they had made. As Mel put it, "I have fifty, sixty people in the church who are my friends, and only two or three outside."

Insight?

It is not too difficult to fit things together here, is it? The Amazing Believers were fearful, and their religion brought them security. They were unhappy, and now they are overjoyed. Their lives were purposeless, going nowhere, sometimes almost out of control, and religion gave them direction and discipline. They were lonely, and they found friendship and love. In short, the ABs usually had serious emotional difficulties and shortfalls, and conversion solved their problems.

COULD YOU GO BACK?

Could these people ever go back to their nonreligious lives? Five thought it "unlikely" and seventeen "very unlikely." Similarly, the ABs had no difficulty brushing us off when we played the devil's advocate, trying to coax them away from the "bosom of Abraham."

Some of our Amazing Believers had trouble even thinking about the possibility that they might reverse course again. A few said something like, "I am too afraid of death" or "I would feel too guilty if I stopped being religious." But most said that they liked their current lives better, and going back would mean that they would have to give up everything that mattered to them now. They had made a commitment to God and themselves; there was no turning back.

ADVICE TO A BUDDING AMAZING BELIEVER

We asked our Amazing Believers to imagine that a person much like their younger selves came to them with questions about religion. What would they say? *None* of them said outright that the questioner should study both sides of the issue, and then decide whether to become religious or stay nonreligious. Victor came closest to suggesting such a two-sided approach when he responded, "The person should try Christianity, and if that was not the answer, then try something else." And Mel acknowledged that "not every successful person, or happy person, is a religious person."

But the solid majority of the ABs wanted the young person to become Christian. Only Jill, Victor, and Xavier left *that* question open. While all the ABs would probably agree that the questioner ultimately has to decide, the advice they would give would almost always lead to a one-sided search for the truth.

They disagreed instead on how "pushy" to be. At one end of the scale, Art, Heather, and Nora would encourage questioners to study different faiths to find the right one for them. Cam, Mel, Ulla, and Wendy wanted the person to become a Christian, but indicated they would be pretty laid back. Cam said he would try to become the young person's friend, as did Bev, Ken, and Mel. Ed, Gil, Ivan, and Pam would attempt to get the person into a youth group or Bible camp. Most of the rest would ask to pray with questioners, read the Bible to them, or send them to a minister. Frieda and Orson seemed ready to preach to the potential convert.

How Would You Raise Your Children?

Of the thirteen ABs we interviewed in 1995, Art, Heather, Jill, and Laura said they would *not* give their children a religious upbringing beyond "having a Bible around the house" or teaching there is a God. The other nine would take their children to church and give them definite religious training. But Cam, Pam, and Xavier would let their children make the decision about their religious beliefs when they got older. The other ABs did not mention such a possibility.

The "Real" Amazing Believers

At the beginning of this chapter we noted that ten of the Amazing Believers (Bev, Cam, Diane, Frieda, Ivan, Ken, Mel, Orson, Pam, and Wendy) were much more active religiously than the other fourteen. If one decided they were the only "real" converts to Christ, what would an analysis of just their cases reveal?

In a nutshell, they epitomize most of the trends mentioned above. As you would expect, they had very high Christian Orthodoxy scores (mean of 212.4 versus 201.2 for the other ABs). But they placed especially high on the measure of authoritarianism, with a mean of 173.3, versus 121.3 for the other ABs (who are quite normal in this respect). All but Diane had experienced serious emotional problems before conversion (and Diane had certainly been shaken by death). All but Diane were brought to Christianity by peers, through youth groups and so on. All but Ivan attended a fundamentalist Protestant church. All their younger selves would have been shocked by their transformation, saying things like "F— off!" "You're crazy!" "You're wasting my time!" and "Leave me alone!" All felt wonderfully blessed by their conversion. All but Cam and Orson were "B+" students in high school or worse; in fact, they generally had the lowest grades of the Amazing Believers. All but Cam and Mel said they would try hard to convert a wondering adolescent. All who served in our 1995 study definitely planned to give their children a religious upbringing. In short, almost everything we found about the twenty-four ABs would "go double" for the most active Amazing Believers. They provided the solid core of the findings.[3]

So much, then, for the Amazing Believers. They proved exceedingly rare, and you could argue that our nets landed two varieties, not one: those who are religiously active, and those whose new beliefs did not spark much of a religious response. If you want to talk solely about the first variety, then we found ten in about four thousand students at our universities. Even if you keep all the Amazing Believers you catch, as "fishers of men," they amount to less than 1 percent of the student body. Which is all the more reason to value the information they gave us about themselves.

To tell you a little secret, we thought the Amazing Apostates' stories would prove more interesting than those of the Amazing Believers. We were wrong. The ABs had more drama and a stronger "finish"—especially if you like redemption at the end of a narrative. While the AAs' decisions often brought them pain, the "moment of truth" for them could have taken place in a library. But the AB stories were set in bars, at funerals, or in the Bible. What other differences did you spot? We think there are many, and offer them for your consideration in the next chapter.

NOTES

1. See, for example, Batson, Schoenrade and Ventis (1993), and Levin, Taylor and Chatters (1994).

2. As noted in note 5 of chapter 3, university admission standards differ for the authors' respective institutions. Since Wilfrid Laurier University required high school grades of "B+" or higher for most of its programs, it was unusual for its students to carry many C's or D's on their high school transcripts. One below average student did appear, however: an individual who was admitted as a "mature student" rather than through the regular admission procedure. The University of Manitoba allows more general access to its programs, and thus has more variable grades among its entering students. But the twelve Manitoba ABs also included several mature students with poor academic histories.

3. Many of our findings concerning ABs parallel a much more general literature on "sudden conversion" (as opposed to more gradual conversion). This literature suggests that such conversions

are often preceded by crises in people's lives, typically involving personal problems and conflicts, whether or not the convert comes from a religious background. Further, converts have been characterized as seeking security or escape, and they perceive a need to gain control over their crises. Finally, our ABs' feelings of happiness and satisfaction have also been noted more generally among converts. (See, for example, Hood et al., 1996, for a summary of this literature.)

6

A Comparison of Amazing Apostates and Amazing Believers

We began this book by noting that Amazing Apostates and Amazing Believers confound both common sense and our socialization theories. They did not grow up "as the twig was bent," but instead headed in completely opposite directions. This hardly ever happens. Did it occur for the same reason in both cases? Did both groups carry a "Reverse Socialization" gene? Or are AAs and ABs very different people, who went their diametrically opposed ways for completely different reasons? Let's compare and contrast their cases.[1]

SURVEY SCORES

The differences we found in AA and AB answers to the twenty Questions and twenty Doubts make sense, don't they? You

208

would expect apostates to have a lot more of both. But the big gap on the Right-Wing Authoritarianism scale gives us pause. The AAs had an average score of 93.7, considerably lower than the sample mean of 123.8. Most of them (26) placed in the bottom *quarter* of the overall sample in authoritarianism scores, making them "Low RWAs." On the other hand, the ABs averaged 141.7, and fully half of them were "High RWAs."[2]

The Amazing Believers cannot consider this part of the "Good News." As mentioned in chapter 3, RWA scale scores have been widely and consistently linked to many "pre-fascist" behaviors, including aggression against quite a variety of victims, prejudice, supporting abuse of power by officials, hypocrisy, conformity, and dogmatism.[3] While an average score of 141.7 is *not* high in the overall scheme of things, and arose partly because some items on the RWA scale mention religion, the overall difference between AAs and ABs remains striking. And we should recall that the "real" (i.e., actively involved) Amazing Believers had an average RWA score of 173.3, which *is* high in the scheme of things.

A certain amount of evidence (Altemeyer, 1988) indicates that religious training tends to produce authoritarian people, which would lead to the prediction that AAs will be *more* authoritarian than ABs, since they had many more years of religious training. But we also think that authoritarianism develops into a personality trait during adolescence, not earlier. So we suspect Amazing Apostates usually became much less authoritarian during their teens, while Amazing Believers became more so, primarily because of their respective movements away from, and toward, religion.

DEMOGRAPHIC VARIABLES

Our studies turned up almost no big differences here. AAs were a little more likely to be men, and ABs tended to be women. This fits a general finding about apostates and believers. Firstborns tended to show up a little more than expected in both groups, which does not fit a general finding. Both groups had a median age of nineteen at the time of the interview, with a few "geezers" almost as old as the investigators appearing for variety.

Two background differences show up in the interviews, however. First, divorce was over three times as prevalent in AB families as in apostates'. Other AB families seemed troubled, or else cold and indifferent. AAs generally came from happier circumstances. Second, in terms of denominational background, we noted that the Catholic church lost more of its "well-raised" youth than any other faith. It only made one AB conversion in return. By contrast, the fundamentalist Protestant churches came out ahead in the exchange. Despite the fact that Amazing Believers were about twice as rare overall as Amazing Apostates, these churches gained more ABs than they lost AAs.

AGES AT WHICH THE CHANGE OCCURRED

Amazing Apostates began to change appreciably sooner, at age 12.5 years on the average versus 16.2 for the Amazing

Believers.[4] It also took them over twice as long to make the transition, some three years versus a year and a half. We think these numbers tell quite a story.

AAs tended to begin questioning their religion at the onset of adolescence, when young people start questioning a lot of things. Their edifice of religious beliefs then began to come apart, brick by brick, until finally the whole design came crashing down. This took a fair bit of time precisely because it took place step by step. AAs also had no reason to hurry, and the decision to abandon the family religion was usually daunting. Still most Amazing Apostates had abandoned their religion before most Amazing Believers had even begun to take their places in the ranks.

If questions arose in the minds of ABs at the onset of adolescence, they apparently led nowhere. It took them until the age of sixteen on the average to become interested in religion because it usually required a while for the personal problems in their lives to become serious. Once that had happened, it took so little time for them to make the switch, in comparison with the AAs, because they *were* in a bigger hurry and they were not daunted by the possibility of a hostile family reaction.

So the Amazing Believers almost never seemed to convert step by step. They did not first decide there was a God, next figure out the attributes that an almighty being would have, then study the evidence for life after death, and so on. Instead they just decided after a certain exposure to Christianity, sometimes suddenly, to adopt the whole faith—whatever it was. This was usually based upon acceptance of a central tenet, such as that in the well-publicized scriptural passage John 3:16: "For God so loved the world, that he gave his only begotten Son, that whosoever believeth in him should not perish, but have everlasting life." *After* that acceptance,

ABs often devoted themselves to discovering the rest of their new beliefs by studying the Bible, joining discussion groups, and so on.

REASONS FOR THE CHANGE

By and large, Amazing Apostates and Amazing Believers switched places for quite different reasons. AAs almost always changed because they felt intellectually compelled to do so. They could no longer believe in God, in the Bible, and in most of the other teachings of their faith. This is interesting, for we saw in chapter 1 that religion generally does a good job answering questions about God's existence and the Bible. But despite all the pressures on them, the AAs found too many inconsistencies, too many unprovens, too many implausibilities—and also too much sexism and too much unfairness—to base their lives any longer on what they came to see as a pack of fables. They had an unusual drive for the truth and personal integrity. We think that drive was put there by the most distinctive feature of their upbringing, their strong religious training.

The Amazing Apostates often said they wanted to hold onto the beliefs of their youth, but reason gave them no choice. The Amazing Believers, in contrast, now feel those same beliefs are the most profound truths in the universe. However, they appear to have accepted Christianity not because reason gave them no choice, but because conversion solved big emotional problems. Most of all, they were frightened; others battled loneliness and depression. Religion provided security, joy, purpose, self-discipline, fellowship, and love. When that emotional salvation was absent in ABs, so was dedication.

FAMILY REACTIONS

Nearly all of the AAs felt guilty or fearful about doubting the family religion. Still, they frequently went to their parents for guidance with their first questions, even though the parents' initial reaction could be quite negative. In contrast, almost none of the ABs felt any guilt or fear about questioning the family *non*religion, but they still only told their mothers and fathers after they had made their decision. This probably reflects the difference in the family backgrounds.

Understandably, the AAs had a much more difficult time with their families than the ABs did. When questioning the home religion caused big problems, they usually "dummied up" but continued to change nonetheless. We have suggested that the more parents stress the family religion, the more they may unwittingly keep their children from coming to them when questions arise.

The loss of contact between the two generations in the AA cases strikes us as particularly sad because the apostates were usually not rebelling against their parents per se, or becoming critical of things in general. And as far as we could tell, they usually had not abandoned most of the morals they had been taught. But when they rejected their parents' basic religious beliefs, they caused their mothers and fathers, and themselves, much pain.

We thought the Amazing Believers would pay a similar price, because we imagined they would have fiercely atheistic parents. But they did not; nobody cried when the ABs announced their change. So while the AAs created emotional problems for themselves when they changed, the ABs got rid of theirs.

THE DIFFERENT ROLE OF PEERS

It appeared in some cases that Amazing Believers' parents did not object to their children's religious conversion because they did not particularly care about them. That isolation in families where "nobody talks much about anything" probably created these ABs' loneliness and led them to their peers for comfort.

The peer groups played very different roles for the AAs and ABs. One may seriously doubt whether most of the Believers would have converted without the interest and guidance of their friends. Few ABs had picked up a Bible and become Christians simply because of what they read. Instead the churches should feel well served by their youth groups, summer camps and retreats, where religion was introduced in a social setting featuring committed peers. The future ABs almost always went for social reasons, not to learn about religion.

In contrast, the AAs usually discussed religion with their believing and nonbelieving friends because they were trying to find the answers that adults had not been able to provide. But almost none of the apostates was "converted" by peers or anyone else. They basically did it as individuals, with no social encouragement. There are few atheist-sponsored summer camps or youth groups.

COSTS AND GAINS

Amazing Apostates undoubtedly had their regrets. They had often paid a heavy price for their apostasy: alienation from their families and loss of friends. We also noted that they almost never volunteered they were happier. Instead they observed—often wistfully—that they had thrown away their guide to life, a way of understanding everything. Now they were on their own, having to find a meaning in life and facing inevitable death at the end. But most AAs thought the upside to this situation justified all. They were their own person now, they could stake out their own identity, they were freer, more open-minded, and they had been strong enough to do a very difficult thing.

Interestingly, virtually none of the ABs counted such psychological achievements among their new blessings. If AAs rejoiced in being independent, ABs were glad to be part of a strong group. If AAs cherished control over their own destiny, ABs depended on their religion to help control *them*. If AAs now felt self-confident, ABs placed their confidence in the Lord. If AAs felt strong, ABs knew they were weak on their own.

In retrospect, we can see that the AAs knowingly *abandoned* the very things that appealed most to the ABs, such as security, guidance, fellowship, and especially a promise of life after death. We saw in chapter 1 that questions about

215

death arise more than any other as young people think about religion. We also saw that religion usually does a good job answering these questions. Amazing Believers embraced those answers; Amazing Apostates walked away.

Whether you think the AAs were mighty right or mighty foolish, you have to admit they were courageous and committed to "finding the truth, whatever it is." But if they are stronger than the ABs, we have to remember they generally came from better circumstances and had a lot fewer problems in life.

INTELLECTUAL ACHIEVEMENT

Part of the reason Amazing Apostates had been able to leave their religion, part of the reason they probably had such confidence in their judgment, was that they were usually very bright. Most of them had been "A" students in high school, often the brightest person in their class. Faith could seem a cop-out to those who had been rewarded all their lives for being able to figure things out. Bright students would also be more likely to find inconsistencies in religious teachings, and require proofs for religious beliefs as they were accustomed to providing them for theorems in geometry and the laws of physics.

Some of the Amazing Believers were just as bright, but most of them had not done as well in school. (We are not saying they were stupid; after all, they were students at a university.) And the academically bright ABs tended to be the "theoretical Christians" who never went to church. We noted ABs did not convert to Christianity for intellectual reasons, but seemingly for emotional ones, and they seemed content to accept things on faith rather than reason. As Pam put it, "I'm pretty accepting of things. I don't push them away because they're stupid. . . . Like the Bible. Most people think it's just a bunch of stories. But they deal with life. They can help you with whatever is wrong."

CERTAINTY THAT THEY WILL NOT GO BACK

Both groups felt they had done the right thing and would never go back to their old ways.[5] Consequently, both AAs and ABs were unimpressed when we suggested they might be better off if they went back to their previous beliefs. A few of the apostates seem to have dropped their religion for rather superficial reasons, and a couple of the believers seem unsure of their new footing. But we would be surprised if many of these students reversed the new direction in their lives.

ADVICE TO A YOUNG QUESTIONER

We *were* surprised by the answers we got to our question about helping a youth searching for the truth about religion. We expected both groups to say, "Well, I'd try to convince him to believe what I do." And the Amazing Believers usually did. But virtually none of the Amazing Apostates wanted to steer the person to the path they had taken. Instead—in sharp contrast to the ABs—they said over and over again, "Investigate both sides of the question, then decide." In fact the AAs were more likely to recommend talking to parents, or a minister, than to say, "Go read what atheists say."

We do not think this happened because apostates "don't believe in anything, and so have nothing to recommend." They believe in a great deal, and at the minimum they could take a young questioner through all their reasons for rejecting traditional religious teachings. But one of the things in which they clearly believe is the right of the individual to make up his own mind. And so they said many times, "I would not want to sway the person one way or the other."

Should we condemn the Amazing Believers, then, for wanting to steer young questioners to Christianity? Well, suppose you had discovered the perfect way to live life, a way that solved all your problems and promised you an eternity of happiness. Would it not be selfish to keep the news to yourself? One can argue whether the ABs have actually discovered what they think they have, just as one can debate whether the AAs did the right thing. But given the Believers' backgrounds, it must certainly seem to them that they have found the key to life. And so they would send the seeker on a one-sided search, just as we saw in chapter 1 that persons with strong religious roots engaged primarily in one-sided searches when questions about religion arose in their own minds.

RAISING THEIR OWN CHILDREN

Just as we were surprised by the Amazing Apostates' responses to our "young seeker" question, we were also caught off-guard by their answers to our question about how they would raise their own children. Most of them said they would either send their kids to church, or else not oppose their children learning about religion from grandparents, friends, and so on. Their overwhelming stand was again, "Let them find out both sides, and decide for themselves." Some of the AAs also believed that, whatever its other drawbacks, religious training gives young people many good things.

The Amazing Believers also surprised us a little here, as about 30 percent of them said they would *not* send their children to church. But these were inactive Christians themselves, and so perhaps their answers were predictable. The active ABs all intended to give their children a strong religious upbringing. In which case one can wonder, will some of their children end up Amazing Apostates some day? And will some of the Amazing Apostates' children end up Amazing Believers instead? Will the flip-flop flop-flip?

THE MANY TWISTS OF SOCIALIZATION

Probably not, in both cases. We have to recall how rare AAs and ABs are, and our interviews show us why. Most people who come from religious backgrounds probably do not find that their religion "comes up short." If high intelligence plays a role in this decision, high intelligence is rare. In addition, some who find the family religion unconvincing may still rightly fear the consequences of breaking away. Besides parental reaction, a good deal of our self-concept is based on our religious affiliation, and, as we saw in the "Back to the Future" fantasies, giving up your religion involves getting a divorce from yourself. Furthermore, people can always "compartmentalize" particular teachings as unbelievable, but still accept the overall system. Abandoning "the religion of your forefathers" is a terribly big step.

If AAs are rare, why are ABs—especially active ABs—even rarer? Why don't more people who grow up with little religious training become believers? For one thing, religious teachings do not seem particularly believable to those raised outside them. Also, religion gets a lot of "bad press" these days. We saw in chapter 1 that the biggest doubts our students had about religion arose from the way it seemed to pressure others, and the intolerance it showed toward various groups.

But also, most people from weak religious backgrounds probably do not end up with the serious problems that our ABs did. Of those who do, some might never be able to obtain *their* divorce from themselves. Others would find support and comfort from their families, nonreligious friends, and professional counselors. Our active ABs almost always came from the particular, peculiar circumstance of deep personal problems that were solved through the intervention of highly religious friends.

In the end, *we think we can understand both Amazing Apostates and Amazing Believers in terms of how they were brought up and what happened to them as they matured. We*

220

think the AAs rejected their religion primarily because their religious training made them care so much about the truth and having integrity. It's not that their upbringing failed; indeed, it worked so well that ultimately the family religion failed the test it helped establish. The ABs turned to God for quite different reasons. Their experiences in life had made them fearful, lonely, and depressed. This was due partly to trouble or indifference in the home, partly to the death of loved ones, partly because of too much drinking and "living in the fast lane." But their conversion is quite understandable if you know what had happened to them in the past, and what they got by becoming religious.

If our Amazing Apostates and Amazing Believers passed each other at some church door, as the former left for good and the latter thanked heaven for having been shown the way in, they probably would think the people heading the other way were making a big mistake. The two groups are very different people now, *but they always were*. The reasons for their opposite futures lie in their very contrasting pasts.

NOTES

1. Two qualifications seem appropriate here. First, we realize that we have only studied university students, and that the factors we have uncovered may not play such a role in other young people. Second, we have been assuming that our interviewees told us the truth. We have no serious doubts about their answers to the questionnaires; the students did not know which pattern of answers could involve them in a further study. But we *do* seriously doubt that their recollections in the interviews were always accurate.

Even when people try to tell you the unvarnished truth about their pasts, they tend to invent their histories to a certain degree because memory fails. So we do not know that searching really began at the ages recalled, for example. But we doubt that the interviews as a whole contain *systematic* distortions that led us down the garden path. The error is probably random, which makes it harder to see clearly what happened, but should not obscure the overall truth.

2. The difference in AA and AB means is statistically significant beyond the .001 level; $t = 5.24$.

3. See Altemeyer (1981, 1988, 1996) for a full review of the literature on the RWA scale.

4. This difference is statistically significant beyond the .001 level, with $t = 3.59$. So also is the difference in how long it took to make the change, with $t = 4.50$.

5. The Amazing Believers' average score on the -2 to +2 scale we used equaled +1.77, while that of the Amazing Apostates was +1.50. The difference is just statistically significant by a two-tailed test, with $t = 2.05$, $p < .05$.

7

Our Findings in a Broader Context

Our excursions into the lives of Amazing Apostates and Amazing Believers might leave the reader wondering how these findings fit into other studies on the "psychology of religion." Psychologists and sociologists have studied religion in thousands of investigations, and some of their conclusions are relevant here. We have referred in passing to some of these throughout the book, but now we shall consider them directly.

First, to the best of our knowledge no one has studied AAs and ABs before. Most research on religion has focused on "religious people," analyzing the ways in which they are religious, how this affects their lives, and so on (for reviews of these studies, see, for example, Batson, Schoenrade and Ventis, 1992; Hood, Spilka, Hunsberger and Gorsuch, 1996; Paloutzian, 1996; Wulff, 1991). We instead selected a much smaller, but very interesting group to study. So we cannot point to any specific investigations of such people in previous work, but merely comment on the relevance of others' findings. We will confine our consideration of other work to four main areas: religious development and socialization (including issues of gender and religious doubt), conversion, apostasy, and authoritarianism.

RELIGIOUS DEVELOPMENT AND SOCIALIZATION

Are Religious Beliefs Genetically Inherited?

Almost a century ago psychologists and others felt that much of our behavior was biologically determined. A "theory of instincts" developed to "explain" much of human behavior, which otherwise seemed inexplicable. It should not surprise us that as social scientists discovered that some form of religion was present in virtually every society they could find, they began to speculate that religion must also be "instinctive." Somehow, they thought, people are "naturally" religious, and this tendency must be passed along through the inheritance process.

These ideas have popped up periodically over the years, in psychological books and papers. For example, the psychoanalyst Carl Jung (1933, 1938) theorized that we humans are driven by a need to find a deity, to believe in a supreme power. "The facts prove, says Jung . . . that the psyche possesses a religious function" (Wulff, 1991, p. 434). David Elkind (1970) felt that as we develop, the natural course of our mental growth lends itself to the development of religiousness. That is, we seem to need to find a spiritual explanation for understanding the world and the universe. More

224

recently, researchers at the University of Minnesota (Bouchard, Lykken, McGue, Segal and Gellegen, 1990; Waller, Kojetin, Bouchard, Lykken and Tellegen, 1990) studied sets of identical twins raised together and others reared apart. These authors concluded that religion does indeed have strong inherited aspects, and that family environment is *not* a very strong influence on children's religiosity.

As much as these "nativistic" explanations appeal to some people, most social scientists are skeptical. The "Minnesota Twins" study, not yet replicated, provides the only solid evidence that religion is inherited. However, the methods and conclusions of these researchers have been criticized by others; for example, the underlying assumption that identical twins reared apart must have been raised in environments with no similarity when other research has indicated there is often considerable environmental similarity (e.g., Dudley, 1991; Beckwish, Geller and Sarkar, 1991).

And the findings reported in this book offer little support for the genetic positions. For example, one wonders how the Amazing Apostates could, if they are "wired" to be religious, take such a deliberate turn away from religion in spite of considerable religious training and pressures to remain religious. It might be argued by a "nativist" that these people must have been "wired" to be nonreligious, but at present we would then seem to be limited to "after-the-fact" explanations: if someone is religious (or nonreligious), it must be because of genetic influence.

Further, why is the emphasis placed on religion in the childhood home such a good predictor of one's current religiousness (see chapter 1)? In many ways, our findings (as well as those of many other researchers) support the common sense socialization explanations of religious development.

225

The Importance of Parental Influence

At the beginning of chapter 1 we challenged readers to think about *why* they believe as they do. We also noted that there is overwhelming evidence that religious beliefs are generally acquired from one's parents[1] and other "social" sources. A recent text on the psychology of religion offered the following conclusion:

> All of the different approaches to studying parental influence in the religious socialization process converge on a single conclusion: Parents play an extremely important role in the developing religious attitudes and practices of their offspring. In fact, few researchers would quarrel with the conclusion that parents are *the* most important influence in this regard. (Hood, Spilka, Hunsberger and Gorsuch, 1996, p. 82)

Usually, this is accomplished by the amount of emphasis parents place on religion in the home. For example, Altemeyer (1988, p. 218) found that the correlation between religious emphasis during youth and continued acceptance of the family religion among over five hundred students was .58. Even the students' parents, who were nearly fifty years old, showed a similar lasting effect (.46) of their own childhood level of religious emphasis.

This basic finding has been replicated many times by different researchers. Quite consistently, parental emphasis placed on religion in the childhood home is related to stronger acceptance of religious teachings as those children grow into adults. Conversely, apostasy is very frequently associated with weak or no emphasis on religion in the home.[2]

226

AAs and ABs and General Research on Religious Acceptance

Let us look at our Amazing Apostates and Amazing Believers to consider how our findings fit into the more general religious socialization literature. We have argued that, in spite of the obvious impression that Amazing Apostates have somehow violated the socialization generalization offered above, they probably do *not* contradict the conclusion that parents strongly influence religious development. Although they have left the religion of their parents, most AAs made it clear to us that they had tried hard to accept parental teachings, but critical analysis of the beliefs led them to conclude that they simply could not accept the basic teachings. The rejection itself had roots in the way they were raised, for they were strongly taught to "believe the truth." When the AAs tried to figure out what the truth was, religion failed the test. The AAs faced up to the implications, often at considerable cost to their lives. Their parents were often upset or angry about their children's loss of faith, the AAs lost the security which religion had given them, and so on. If the parents had taught, "You must follow the Truth no matter what it costs you in this life," their children were simply doing what they had been taught. In this sense then, the AAs *did* accept an important parental teaching, to find and believe the truth.

The real question about the AAs is, why did they try to *figure out* the truth when most children in their circumstances take it as given? We think their intellectual brightness led them to question. They had been rewarded often in the past for figuring out the right answer to things. While some would call them "smart aleks," the point is they *were* smart

227

and they had been trained for many years to have confidence in their intelligence. They had a lot of experience at understanding things others could not see.

Amazing Apostasy and Modeling

In a related vein, some studies have concluded that young children are religious because of "habit" or parental modeling, but that children do not themselves think complexly or critically about religion (see, for example, Allport, 1950). Stage theorists of cognitive development (e.g., Piaget, 1952, 1954) and especially religious cognitive development (e.g., Goldman, 1964) have concluded that before the early teen years, thinking processes are limited and, for example, children are not capable of the complex and abstract thought necessary to understand religion. It is argued that only in early adolescence can one begin to understand the abstractness and complexities of religious beliefs and rituals.

In one sense, our data generally support this approach, since most of our participants' serious questioning and doubting of religion reportedly occurred in the early to mid-teen years. And this is consistent with the common observation that adolescence is a time when many people "rethink" their religious (and other) beliefs—questioning, doubting, and criticizing before deciding what they do and do not believe (Hunsberger et al., 1996).

However, if we are to believe the life stories told to us by our AAs, at least some of these people claim to have been thinking critically about religion *very* early in their lives, even during the preschool years. Of course we have no way of

228

confirming that these memories are accurate, but at least some of our AAs strongly believed that they questioned religious teachings during childhood. Maybe some children are capable of more complex thought about religion than we have sometimes given them credit for.[3]

Amazing Believers

The Amazing Believers also seem at first blush to violate the religious socialization rule. That is, they did end up as "believers" in spite of little if any parental religious influence in their lives. True, some of these students did have at least one parent who was rather positive about religion, and a few had a strongly opposed parent. But most ABs came from families where the parents simply didn't care about religion, or else believed but were quite inactive. Yet the ABs became strongly believing Christians.

We have suggested that other factors may have been influential. Many of the ABs had problems in their lives, and were actively searching for either a solution or an elixir that might ease their pain. In some cases the problems involved the parents themselves (disagreements or major differences with or between the parents, divorce, death, etc.), but in other cases the problems existed apart from the parents. Whatever the source of the difficulties, these people typically found that religion offered them solace, security, and an anchor in their lives. Apparently, the emotional turmoil in many AB lives was enough to prevail over the (in these cases) much weaker socialization pressures to be nonreligious. Also, we must keep in mind that these students were living in a society where religion is widely accepted and endorsed by many people, and thus their embrace of religion was to some extent consistent with societal expectations. In fact, in most cases the ABs' parents were *glad* their children had become religious.

Gender

Many studies have reported that men are less religious than women on average, whether the issue at hand is frequency of prayer or church attendance, interest in religion, or intensity or orthodoxy of beliefs (e.g., Argyle & Beit-Hallahmi, 1975; Batson et al., 1993; Benson et al., 1989; Francis & Wilcox, 1996; Nelsen & Potvin, 1981). Our own results coincide with the generalization that women are more religious than men, since we found a higher number of men who became Amazing Apostates, but more women who became Amazing Believers. Possibly there are socialization pressures for women to be more religious than men, or, as Batson et al. (1993) have suggested, sex role training might involve pressure on women to be more submissive and nurturing, traits which might be seen as being associated with greater religiousness, and which might also be more likely to incline one to become an AB rather than an AA.[4]

Doubt

For some reason, there has been little research over the years on issues of religious questioning and doubt. The few papers that have considered this issue have tended to focus on classifying types of doubt (e.g., Allport, 1950; Grant, 1974; Helfaer, 1972; Hunsberger et al., 1993) and how doubt is linked to the complexity of one's thinking about religious and other issues (Hunsberger et al., 1993; Hunsberger et al., 1996). The findings in this book suggest that doubt plays an important role in the apostasy process of AAs, from the appearance of questions relatively early in life to the emergence of serious religious doubts by early to mid-adolescence.

The role of doubt in religious development deserves greater attention. Why don't most people experience *more* doubt? Why do some people, as we saw in chapter 1, undertake a broad-ranging, two-sided search for answers to their religious concerns, while others settle for a cursory, one-sided search for answers to their (apparently less serious) questions? And how can the same doubts lead to opposite resolutions by AAs and ABs? For example, serious illness or death seems to direct some people toward religion (e.g., Art, Diane, and Ken), while ultimately pushing others away from religion (e.g., Frank, Betty, and Nancy). We have much to learn about the role of religious doubt in people's lives.

CONVERSION

Traditionally, studies have divided conversion experiences into those that are "sudden" and those that are more "gradual." The "sudden" paradigm seems to be modeled after Paul's conversion on the road to Damascus. This type of conversion typically occurs during adolescence, and is said to be more emotional than rational, involving external influences acting on a passive recipient and resulting in a dramatic transformation of self which is "permanent" (Hood et al., 1996; Richardson, 1985). Gradual conversions also are thought to lead to "a transformation of self within a religious context" (Hood et al., p. 281), but tend to occur a bit later in life (late adolescence or early adulthood), involve a more active role by the convert, a deliberate search for meaning and purpose, entail intellectual and rational processes, and result in a more "passionate theology" (Hood et al., 1996; Richardson, 1985).

This very simplified version of sudden versus gradual conversions bears a striking resemblance to differences we found between ABs and AAs. Our ABs generally had "faster" conversions (about a year and a half, compared to AAs' three years), accompanied by strong emotional overtones arising from crises in their lives. They also tended to be relatively passive, "worked on" by friends, romantic interests, and so on. And of course the ABs also reported dramatic changes in their lives. Thus, our Amazing Believers reproduced the classic pattern of sudden conversions that has appeared in the psychological literature for a hundred years (e.g., Coe, 1916; James, 1902/1985; Leuba, 1896; Pratt, 1920).

Similarly, our picture of the Amazing Apostate bears a striking resemblance to some of the characteristics outlined for gradual converts—although the AAs "converted" to atheism. For example, the process of becoming an AA is strongly intellectual and rational, and seems to result from a slow, careful search for meaning and purpose. It, too, ultimately results in a dramatic transformation of self in terms of "becoming one's own person" and being free and confident in one's (non)religious beliefs. In some ways then, the departure

232

of our AAs from the religion of their parents reminds us of the gradual conversion process described in previous studies.

APOSTASY

A substantial literature has accumulated over the past thirty years on the general phenomenon of "apostasy," or abandoning one's religious affiliation to become "nonreligious." Some of the early work on apostates characterized them as rebellious misfits who had rejected their social community generally, as well as reacted against parental and religious teachings. These people were supposedly maladjusted, had radical leftist political orientations, got along poorly with their parents, and displayed a decidedly intellectual orientation to life. Caplovitz and Sherrow (1977) even used a disease analogy to suggest that these factors somehow were analogous to "germs" which infected their hosts with a predisposition toward apostasy.

Other work has generally not confirmed this overall picture of apostasy (see, e.g., Hunsberger, 1983; Hunsberger & Brown, 1984; Kotre, 1971; Nelsen, 1981; Wuthnow & Mellinger, 1978). In fact, as we pointed out in chapter 3, many apostates may be much better described by the concept of "drift," since they seem simply to be drifting a bit farther away from the religion of their (already relatively nonreligious) parents. That is, there never was any strong religious modeling or training provided by the parents or anyone else in most apostates' lives, and their religious affiliation before defection was marginal, at best. It should not surprise us that these adolescents and young adults do not have any religious affiliation. In this sense, most apostates are showing more consistency with parental (non)religiousness than rebellion and rejection.

But the AAs in our study were selected precisely because they *did* have strong religious modeling and training in their childhood homes, and there was considerable pressure for them to become very religious people. And our Amazing Apostates bear little resemblance to the apostates of the mainstream literature. They had hardly "drifted" into non-belief, but instead had made a "break" so sharp you could almost hear it snap, crackle, and pop. Are they the disgruntled apostates of legend? We did find a strong intellectual/rational orientation among our AAs, but they showed little evidence of political radicalism, maladjustment, or the poor relationships with parents claimed by Caplovitz and Sherrow.

A number of sociological studies of apostates have been based on national opinion polls of Americans, and have suggested that apostates in general "tend to be younger, more affluent, predominantly male, more educated, more committed to new morality values, less happy, and less confident in American institutions than nonapostates" (Hadaway, 1989, p. 202). These tendencies have been supported by the findings of some other studies (e.g., Roof & Hadaway, 1977; Roof & McKinney, 1987). In our investigations we began with a relatively homogeneous pool of university students, and then examined the factors which seem to distinguish (amazing) apostates from (amazing) believers. Therefore, differences in age, education, and so on have little relevance to our investigation. Rather, we have focused on the differences apparent between AAs and ABs *other* than basic sociodemographic factors. Our Amazing Apostates did seem to be less "happy" than the ABs, possibly because they felt their apostasy had "cost" them a lot (parental respect, religious friends, etc.), whereas the Amazing Believers had a long list of gains from their conversion, many of which sounded very much like forms of "happiness."[5]

RELIGIOUSNESS AND AUTHORITARIANISM

As we have noted at several points, research has found connections between people's religiousness and the extent to which they have *authoritarian follower* ("High RWA") personalities. We shall describe some of these findings now, but first we should distinguish between leaders and followers in authoritarian systems. To cite an extreme example: if you think of the Nuremberg rallies, Hitler and the Nazi elite on the podium would be authoritarian leaders, while the masses of ardent Nazis filling the stadium would be authoritarian followers. We do not find many Hitlers or Nazi supporters in our studies, but some people do score much higher than average on tests that measure these two kinds of authoritarian personalities.[6]

Dictator-type personalities naturally show a strong drive for personal power and dominance. They also admit they can be mean, cold-blooded, and ruthless. They say they will destroy anyone who blocks their plans. Authoritarian leaders also tend to be relatively amoral, holding that there is no right and wrong, only "what you can get away with." They think it very important to know how to lie convincingly. They believe "there's a sucker born every minute" and smart people learn how to take advantage of them. As you would suspect, then, dictator-types are not usually religious, saying "religion is for suckers." But they will pretend to be devout when it suits their purpose, holding that "the best reason for belonging to a church is to project a good image and have contact with some of the important people in your community."

Authoritarian *followers* by contrast tend to be the truest believers in their religions, the most faithful church-attenders, the most frequent pray-ers, the most dutiful scripture readers. We are not saying all devout persons are right-wing authoritarians, any more than we would suggest your parish priest or minister is an authoritarian leader. But study after study has found High RWAs concentrated in the ranks of the orthodox in religion after religion.

Why should this connection exist? Well, to some extent authoritarian following helps produce religiousness. High RWAs are very submissive to the authorities in their lives. If their authorities teach a certain ideology, they will tend to embrace it. (Hence High RWAs in the Soviet Union tended to be the most ardent Communists.) But to varying degrees religions also promote authoritarian following, teaching their members to submit to religious and even civic authority. So *in general* right-wing authoritarianism and religiousness go together because, within limits, the two reinforce each other. This has proven true in studies of Hindus, Jews, and Muslims—as well as Christians—thus far.[7]

If authoritarian followers are more likely to have copied their beliefs from others than to have worked things out for themselves, how might that affect their religious behavior? For one thing, their ideas could be more inconsistent, more self-contradictory, because they have not critically examined their beliefs very much. Their thinking may similarly show

236

lots of double standards. They could prove more dogmatic than most people, because they reached their conclusions largely before they considered the evidence; their only refuge in the face of disconfirming facts may be dogmatism. They may also be readier than most people to accept invalid "evidence" that supports them. They may rely more upon social support for maintaining their beliefs, such as associating with people of like mind.

All these notions could prove false. But experiments have shown that High RWAs do act in these ways. Studies also reveal that authoritarian followers are likely to be "suckered" by insincere politicians or TV evangelists who tell High RWAs what they want to hear. Exploitive authoritarian leaders probably find out quickly who some of the "suckers" are, and authoritarian followers become their first, if not last, victims.

Research has uncovered another worrisome connection between authoritarian leaders and followers: both are highly prejudiced. In fact, most prejudiced persons appear to be one kind of authoritarian or the other. We can easily see why the dictator-types are so hostile toward racial and ethnic minorities. "Inferior groups" provide outlets for their need to dominate and for their meanness. But why should the followers be so prejudiced, too? And does this extend to religious people? Are they more prejudiced than most?

Many studies have found that persons who belong to a religion are, as a group, more prejudiced than those who belong to none.[8] But how can this be, since one knows so many religious people who seem quite *un*prejudiced? The answer turns out not to involve the strength of a person's religious beliefs so much as his *beliefs about those beliefs*. Some people think their religion is fundamentally better than any other in the world, that it contains the fundamental, never-mistaken truths about God and humanity, that this truth is fundamentally opposed by evil forces, and that those who believe in this truth have a fundamentally special relationship with God.

A Religious Fundamentalism scale was developed to measure these attitudes, and such fundamentalism proved to be the source of the religion-prejudice connection. Many people strongly believe their religion, but they do not take such an ethnocentric view of their faith compared with all others, and they tend not to be prejudiced. But the more you think it is fundamentally Us versus Them, and Us is the good guys, the more you look down on Them.[9]

In conclusion, let us recognize that if such findings put religion in a poor light, other studies have been more heartening. For example, religiously committed college students recalled volunteering more hours as tutors, relief workers, and campaigners for social justice than other students did.[10] So it would be as fundamentally wrong to see religion as inherently bad as it is to see religion as fundamentally perfect—fundamentally speaking. The challenge is to increase its good effects, which we sorely need, and lessen the unfortunate ones.

NOTES

1. The evidence on this point is quite extensive. The reader might consult reviews of this literature by Batson et al. (1993), Hood et al. (1996), or Hyde (1990). See also our discussion of these issues, and the relevant literature in note 2, chapter 1.

2. For more information on these issues, the reader might consult Albrecht, Cornwall and Cunningham (1988), Hunsberger

(1976, 1980, 1983, 1985), Hunsberger and Brown (1984), Hood et al. (1996), Kotre (1971), and Ozorak (1989).

3. We might note here a common misconception that religious development and moral development are closely related. That is, in spite of the widespread assumption that morality will not develop in the absence of institutional religion, the related research suggests that the two are actually quite independent. Lawrence Kohlberg, who spent much of his career studying moral development, concluded that it is a fallacy to think that:

> basic moral principles are dependent upon a particular religion, or any religion at all. We have found no important differences in development of moral thinking between Catholics, Protestants, Jews, Buddhists, Moslems, and atheists. Children's moral values in the religious area seem to go through the same stages as their general moral values. . . . Both cultural values and religion are important factors in selectively elaborating certain themes in the moral life but they are not unique causes of the development of basic moral values. (Kohlberg, 1980, pp. 33–34)

4. A similar line of thinking has led some researchers (e.g., Francis & Wilcox, 1996; Thompson, 1991) to conclude that gender orientation, rather than sex per se, contributes to differential religiosity for men versus women.

5. It has been argued that this appearance of happiness among converts is misleading. Rather, it has been suggested that religious people are saying what they are expected to say, since admitting to little happiness is akin to admitting that one's religion has failed. Nonreligious people, on the other hand, may simply be more honest about their feelings, having no religion to defend by claiming "false happiness" (Ellis, 1996). If our Amazing Believers are not genuinely happier now than they were in their prereligious days, they certainly fooled us.

6. The "leader" kind of authoritarian is measured by the

239

Social Dominance Orientation scale developed by Pratto, Sidanius, Stallworth and Malle (1994), and the "follower" by the Right-Wing Authoritarianism scale (Altemeyer, 1996). See Altemeyer (1998) for studies of the authoritarian leader personality and Altemeyer (1996, 1988) for research on the authoritarian follower.

7. See Altemeyer (1996), Altemeyer & Hunsberger (1992), Hunsberger (1996).

8. See Hunsberger (1995) for a review of this research.

9. The Religious Fundamentalism scale (Altemeyer & Hunsberger, 1992) contains such items as, "God has given humanity a complete, unfailing guide to happiness and salvation, which must be totally followed" and "Of all the people on this earth, one group has a special relationship with God because it believes the most in his revealed truths and tries the hardest to follow his laws." Responses to its twenty items usually correlate about .35 on the average, producing alphas of .91 or higher. Its scores correlate about .70 with the Right-Wing Authoritarianism scale.

10. See Batson et al. (1993), Benson et al. (1980), Hood et al. (1996), and Hunsberger & Platonow (1986).

8

Further Studies on Related Matters

We shall conclude with four studies of "normal people's" acceptance or rejection of religion. In the first investigation, nearly four hundred Manitoba students who had been raised as Christians answered an end-of-survey-question in September 1996 about what might have happened if they had been raised as Hindus, Jews, or Muslims instead. Most (57 percent) of the students checked "I would probably believe in some other religion just as much as I believe in Christianity now." A sizeable number (19 percent), however, thought "I would *probably* believe *less strongly* in some other religion than I believe in Christianity now." And a fervent 13 percent said, "I am *certain* I would believe *less strongly* in some other religion than I believe in Christianity now." (The other 11 percent of the sample, many of whom had rejected Christianity, thought they might believe more strongly in some other religion than they presently believed in Christianity.)

Do you not find interesting the people who said that even

241

if they had been raised in some other religion, they would not have accepted it as much as they accepted Christianity? These students seem to be discounting the power of socialization. But we just considered again in chapter 7 the evidence that establishes the fact—obvious to most—that religious students almost always believe in the faith in which they were raised.

The "I would believe more in Christianity" respondents also seemingly underestimate the power of socialization in non-Christian religions. In our studies, students raised as Hindus, Jews, and Muslims are at least as likely to retain the family religion as Christian-raised students are. So the (19 percent + 13 percent =) 32 percent of the students who thought they would not have accepted Hinduism, etc., as much as they have accepted Christianity are very likely wrong.

Who are these students who, unlike their peers, did not appreciate the role that their upbringing had in shaping their fervor? Religious fundamentalists, by and large. *Most* (54 percent) of the students who scored highly (in the upper quartile) on the Religious Fundamentalism scale thought they would "probably" or "certainly" believe in Christianity more, compared with only 13 percent of the nonfundamentalists (the lower quartile).[1]

While most people might have predicted this, does the following fact lend more insight into "what is really going on here?" The Right-Wing Authoritarianism scale predicted students' reactions to our hypothetical question almost as well as the Religious Fundamentalism scale did: 46 percent of the High RWAs, compared with only 15 percent of the Low RWAs, thought they would believe in Christianity more. We know from other studies that authoritarians are much more likely than most people to think that whatever they have been taught is right and inevitable. In the former Soviet Union, for example, High RWAs tended to be fervent Communists, whereas in the United States they tended to be fervent anti-Communists (Altemeyer, 1996, pp. 122–30). Authoritarians sing loudly the songs they have heard while growing up. But they attribute their beliefs to the rightness of the beliefs themselves. So it is not surprising that the religiously most socialized students said that socialization is not all that decisive, because they do not grasp how decisive it has been in their lives. Their "learning" has been so thorough that they do not realize it has been thoroughly learned.

WHY IS THERE STILL RELIGION?

Some philosophers and scientists have asked, "Why is there still religion?" (see, e.g., Bergman, 1996). It seems to them that religious beliefs have been discredited and even disproved so often, people should have stopped leaping for faiths long ago.

The results of our Amazing Believer interviews suggested one answer at least: if a religion endures, it is probably satisfying important human needs, especially emotional ones—whether the beliefs in the religion are true or false. Philosophy and science, by contrast, probably give little such succor, whatever their other merits.

We tested this in September 1996 by asking over five hundred students' parents to indicate, on our usual 0–6 basis, "to what extent do traditional religious beliefs bring you *happiness, joy, and comfort* in the following ways":

243

1. They tell me the purpose of my life. (2.93)
2. They help me deal with personal pain and suffering. (3.20)
3. They take away the fear of dying. (2.93)
4. They tell me what is right and wrong. (3.56)
5. They provide an anchor that keeps me from going astray. (3.22)
6. They explain the mysteries of life. (2.55)
7. They help me control evil impulses. (2.84)
8. They have provided satisfying answers to all the questions in life. (2.32)
9. They make me feel safe in the protection of God. (3.31)
10. They reveal how I can spend all of eternity in heaven with God. (3.11)
11. They bring me closer together with my loved ones. (3.27)
12. They bring me the joy of God's love. (3.30)
13. They tell me I shall rejoin my loved ones after we die. (3.46)
14. They have led me to feel love and support from others. (3.35)
15. They have brought the forgiveness of my sins. (3.23)
16. They protect me against Satan and other evil in this world. (2.71)

While most of these issues involve emotions, you may agree that some of them (e.g., telling right from wrong, explaining mysteries, providing satisfying answers) have significant intellectual aspects.

To provide a basis of comparison, we also asked these parents to answer similar questions about logic and science:

244

"Some people cannot accept traditional religious teachings because they require an act of faith. They base their beliefs instead on logic and science. Would you now indicate to what extent *logic and science* bring you *happiness, joy, and comfort* in each of the following ways."

1. They tell me the purpose of my life. (1.97)
2. They help me deal with personal pain and suffering. (2.26)
3. They take away fear of dying. (1.43)
4. They tell me what is right and wrong. (2.28)
5. They provide an anchor in my life that keeps me from going astray. (2.02)
6. They explain the mysteries of life. (2.53)
7. They help me control evil impulses. (1.73)
8. They have provided satisfying answers to all the questions in life. (2.03)
9. They make me feel safe. (1.91)
10. They reveal how I can live a happy life. (1.96)
11. They serve as a check on my own biases and wrong ideas. (2.42)
12. They bring me the joy of discovery. (3.22)
13. They enable me to work out my own beliefs and philosophies of life. (2.80)
14. They provide the surest path we have to the truth. (2.12)
15. They give the satisfaction of knowing that my beliefs are based upon objective facts and logic, not an act of faith. (2.07)
16. They enable me to search for the truth, instead of just memorizing what others say. (2.81)

The first eight "Joy of Science" items repeated the first eight "Joy of Religion" items. The last eight paralleled certain religious items, or else tried to capture some of the satisfaction that can come from the philosophical or scientific quest.

Results

Overall, the parents indicated that religion brought them significantly more happiness, joy, and comfort than did logic and science. The total score on the sixteen Joys of Religion items equaled 49.3, while that for the Joys of Science came in quite a bit lower, at 35.6.[2]

If you look at the means printed in parentheses after each item above, you will see that most of the religion items averaged over 3.0 ("Moderate joy"—the midpoint of the response scale). While some of these involve basically intellectual concerns, most of the higher scoring items, we submit, speak to emotional comforts. Witness: "They tell me I shall rejoin my loved ones after we die," "They have led me to feel love and support from others," "They bring me the joy of God's love," "They make me feel safe in the protection of God," "They bring me closer together with my loved ones," and "They have brought the forgiveness of my sins."

Only one logic and science item ("They bring me the joy of discovery") had a mean over 3.0. Even more damaging to the philosopher's and scientist's egos, logic and science were not perceived to "provide (more) satisfying answers to all the questions in life" or to "explain the mysteries of life" better than religion did—and this in a rather well-educated sample.

By now you will probably not be surprised to learn that

those who found the greatest joy in religion tended to score highly in Religious Fundamentalism (r = .68) and Right-Wing Authoritarianism (r = .57). But religion brought happiness to many besides these, and science did not.

The last point triggers an obvious criticism of this analysis: the joys of religion can be appreciated by anyone, whereas the joys of logic and science may be available on a more limited basis. So who can be surprised that religion comforts more people than these other paths do?

No one, we imagine, who has spent hours memorizing biology terms or struggling to understand Immanuel Kant. But the original question was, "Why is there still religion?" and the data above show that religion satisfies some important human needs about knowing who we are; why we are here; what will happen to us after we die; how to feel safety, love, and fellowship, and so on. These things logic and science do not do, at least not nearly as well.[3]

We would, as scientists, actually find some joy, happiness, and comfort in science's "poor showing." Science is not supposed to be emotional but objective, dispassionate, and even-handed. (We hope the reader who has gotten to the end of this book is not surprised to hear us say this.) If some scientific theories or discoveries are "beautiful" (such as relativity); or "thrilling" (such as the genetic code), that is pure gravy. The endeavor is based in the cerebral cortex, not the adrenal glands.

But as "Star Trek"'s Dr. McCoy kept telling Mr. Spock, human emotions undeniably enrich our lives and often govern us. They may make us irrational at times, they may cause much of our worst as well as our best behavior. But to ignore them and their role in human enterprise—"That would be illogical."

ACCEPTANCE OR REJECTION OF RELIGION BY MIDDLE ADULTHOOD

Our studies have focused upon the religious decisions made by college freshmen both because they are a convenient group for psychology professors to examine and because they have just emerged from an often turbulent time when they scrutinized the family religion. But will the decisions reached by eighteen-year-olds hold for the rest of their lives? If they have decided to stay in the fold, will they still be found there decades later? If they have decided to chuck the family religion, will they come back to it when they have children of their own?

Speaking as middle-aged adults who once thought that "Fifty is really old," but who now consider fifty "much younger than sixty," we can testify that one's views can change as growth rings accumulate. So maybe youthful decisions to keep or abandon the family religion will be reversed later.

The best answer to the question about long-term changes will come from long-term studies in which groups of people are tracked over the decades. The only longitudinal data we can offer right now come from a study of eighty-six University of Manitoba alumni, who answered a questionnaire for us at the age of thirty-six, about eighteen years after we had surveyed them as freshmen in 1976. Among other things, we asked them how religious they were now, in terms of both beliefs and practice, compared to when they entered college. Overall, very little change was reported. It may be widely thought that people become more religious as they "settle down" after their youthful adventures, but these data do not support this notion.[4]

We *do* have piles of data on the childhood religion and present religion of parents of Manitoba students. Table 1 presents a breakdown of such data from over 2,500 parents surveyed in 1993, 1994, 1995, and 1996. If you run your fingers along the rows and columns of Table 1, the way you do to find the official distance between Chattanooga and Kalamazoo in a road atlas, you can see what happened to the parents who grew up as Anglicans, Catholics and so on by the time they were nearly fifty. You will also find, in the bottom row, the percentage of the present Anglicans, etc., who attended church at least three times per month.

If you study Table I for a minute, you will see that the biggest net "winner" in the transition from home religions to present religions is the "None" category, which tripled in size. Eleven percent of the parents who had been raised Christians had dropped *all* religious identification. While others undoubtedly went through a "disbelieving phase" but then became religious again, the data demonstrate that apostasy often lasts.

The only other category that grew appreciably over the years was generic "Christianity, which nearly tripled. Religious officials cannot be too happy about this either, because these parents had rejected their home religion so much that they no longer considered themselves members of it. They might still believe in God and Jesus, but they identified with no particular church, and most (73 percent) said they never entered one.

Remember from chapter 1 that, overall, our present university students had received less religious educations than their parents had. Who in particular do you think stopped "passing it on"? Largely, one suspects, the parents who became "Nones" and (just) "Christians"—a sizeable group. Do you

249

Table I										
Childhood and Present Religious Identifications of Parents of Manitoba Students										

Raised As:	Present Religion:									
	None	Chris	Angl	Unit	Luth	Menn	Fund	Cath	Jew	Other	Sum
"None"	66	4	3	8	2	3	5	12	0	1	104
"Christian"	16	43	3	9	2	3	3	2	0	0	81
Anglican	47	15	126	32	3	1	11	10	0	2	247
United Ch.*	87	61	17	381	11	2	24	38	1	4	626
Lutheran	24	15	5	14	65	1	5	9	0	1	139
Mennonite	5	10	2	16	3	139	17	4	0	0	196
Fundament.	13	12	0	16	4	1	80	6	1	0	133
Catholic	68	40	12	39	12	2	16	673	1	5	868
Jewish	0	2	0	0	0	0	0	1	50	2	55
Other†	11	4	2	15	0	0	3	10	0	61	106
SUM	337	206	170	530	102	152	164	765	53	76	2555
% who attend church at least 3x/mo.	X	17	16	18	36	80	83	45	13	29	

*The United Church was formed by an amalgamation of the Methodist, Congregationalist, and most Presbyterian churches in Canada in 1925.

†"Other" includes infrequent Christian churches (e.g., Greek Orthodox), Unitarians, Hindus, Muslims, Buddhists, and so on.

think their children will usually become religious later on in their lives, and raise *their* children in a faith? Not likely. The prognosis then: emptier and fewer churches (Bibby, 1993).

But one set of churches grew in these studies: the "fundamentalist Protestants" (which includes Baptists, Pentecostals, Jehovah's Witnesses, the Alliance Church, and so on). True, these religions lost about 40 percent of those who had been raised in them. But they still showed a net increase because they won more than enough converts from other denominations to replace their losses. We shall come back to these conversions in a bit.

All the other faiths lost ground, mostly to "None" and "Christian." Catholicism showed the smallest decline, although 27 percent of the present Catholics were "nominal Catholics" who said they never attended Mass. The Anglican Church shrank the most among the Christian faiths, and shared the unwelcome distinction with the United Church for having the least-attending membership, with about one in six parishioners in the pews most Sundays. At the other extreme, about four of every five Mennonites and fundamentalists attended church "religiously," often more than once a week.

The Reasons for Switching Religions

In the 1995 study, parents who had switched religions were asked to explain why they had done so. The most common reason, given by nearly half (thirty) of the sixty-three responding converts, was "marriage." Sometimes these conversions were pressured, they said, usually by the Catholic church. (Not surprisingly, many of those pressured to convert only switched superficially, and seldom attended church.) But just as often parents said they switched voluntarily so their children would experience just one religion in the home.

The other major reason for switching, mentioned twenty-four times, was active dissatisfaction with the religion in which respondents had been raised. The vast majority (nineteen) of these *deeply* converted joined a fundamentalist Protestant denomination. Why? "A personal belief in Christ was stressed." "It teaches exclusively the Bible." "It is founded on scripture." "The United Church was too liberal and wishy-washy, not committed to absolutes." "I needed to have articles of faith." "The Anglican church does not preach the whole gospel. The Baptist church does; it preaches salvation and the forgiveness of sins in a personal way to all who simply accept Christ as Lord and Savior."

In short, we would suggest, fundamentalism often appealed to these people precisely because it offered definite, simple, written down, absolute, *fundamental* teachings they could count on, instead of the ambiguous, often complicated, frequently argued and (to them) distressingly modifiable principles swirling in their home religions.

It probably takes considerable courage to turn your back on your background, your family, and your friends and join another faith. In a way, the Amazing Apostates show the same courage. But "deep converts," like AAs, and ABs, are rare. Most of the believers in Table 1, most of the way through their lives, still accepted the religion in which they grew up. Which leads to our concluding point. If there is one ultimate, simple, definite, fundamental lesson to be drawn from the studies we have considered in this book, it is this: Do not underestimate the power of socialization when it comes to religion. Even in the cases where it seems socialization has been overthrown, it has just worked in "mysterious ways."

NOTES

1. See note 9 to chapter 7.

2. The difference, with 527 degrees of freedom, is statistically significant beyond the .0001 level. Age among the parents did not correlate significantly with how much joy they received from religion or logic and science. There was a significant but quite small tendency ($r = -.12$) for less educated persons to get more joy from religion. But education did not correlate with happiness derived from logic and science.

The sample contained 278 mothers and 244 fathers, 69 percent of whom lived in cities and who averaged forty-seven years of age and nearly fourteen years of education.

3. This conclusion is further supported by looking at the answers these parents gave to a later question on the survey that sought their "most important outlook or way of understanding things in life." Nine potential answers were offered, such as "A personal outlook all my own" and "The feminist movement." "A religious outlook" was checked off by 175 parents, and their Joys of *Religion* scores averaged 72.9. "A scientific outlook" was specified by 27 others, and their Joys of *Science* scores had a mean of only 50.3. Again, the difference is statistically significant beyond the .0001 level. So first of all, as expected, we found a great deal more people with basically religious outlooks than we did people with scientific ones in this sample. But secondly, religious types derived a lot more happiness from their basic outlook than the scientifically oriented did from theirs.

4. The response scale went from -2 ("Much Less"), through 0 ("The Same"), to +2 ("Much More"). Some individuals said "-2," others said "+ 2," and most landed in between. But the means were just a hair over the "0" mark (0. 17 for beliefs and 0. 18 for practice).

References

Albrecht, S. L., Cornwall, M., and Cunningham, P. H. (1988). Religious leave-taking: Disengagement and disaffiliation among Mormons. In Bromley, D. G. (Ed.), *Falling from the faith: Causes and consequences of religious apostasy* (pp. 62–80). Newbury Park, Calif.: Sage.

Allport, G. W. (1950). *The individual and his religion.* New York: Macmillan.

Altemeyer, B. (1981). *Right-wing authoritarianism.* Winnipeg: University of Manitoba Press.

———. (1988). *Enemies of freedom: Understanding right-wing authoritarianism.* San Francisco: Jossey-Bass.

———. (1996). *The authoritarian specter.* Boston: Harvard University Press.

———. (1998, in press). The other "authoritarian personality." In Zanna, M. (Ed.). *Advances in experimental social psychology,* vol. 32. New York: Academic Press.

Altemeyer, B., & Hunsberger, B. (1992). Authoritarianism, reli-

255

gious fundamentalism, quest, and prejudice. *International Journal for the Psychology of Religion*, 2, 113–33.

Argyle, M., & Beit-Hallahmi, B. (1975). *The social psychology of religion*. London: Routledge & Kegan Paul.

Bahr, H. M., & Albrecht, S. L. (1989). Strangers once more: Patterns of disaffiliation from Mormonism. *Journal for the Scientific Study of Religion*, 28, 180–200.

Batson, C. D., Schoenrade, P., and Ventis, W. L. (1993). *Religion and the individual: A social-psychological perspective*. New York: Oxford.

Beckwith, J., Geller, L., and Sarkar, S. (1991). [Untitled letter to the editor] *Science*, 252, 191.

Benson, P. L., Dehority, J., Garman, L., Hanson, E., Hochschwsender, M., Lebold, C., Rohr, R., and Sullivan, J. (1980). Intrapersonal correlates of nonspontaneous helping behavior. *Journal of Social Psychology*, 110, 87–95.

Benson, P. L., Donahue, M. J., and Erickson, J. A. (1989). Adolescence and religion: A review of the literature from 1970 to 1986. *Research in the social scientific study of religion*, 1, 153–81.

Bergman, G. R. (1996). Religious beliefs of scientists: A survey of the research. *Free Inquiry*, 16 (3), 41–46.

Bibby, R. W. (1993). *Unknown gods: The ongoing story of religion in Canada*. Toronto: Stoddart.

Bouchard, R. J., Jr., Lykken, D. T., McGue, M., Segal, N. L., and Tellegen, A. (1990). Sources of human psychological differences: The Minnesota study of twins reared apart. *Science*, 250, 223–50.

Caplovitz, D., & Sherrow, F. (1977). *The religious drop-outs: Apostasy among college graduates*. Beverly Hills, Calif.: Sage.

Coe, G. A. (1916). *The psychology of religion*. Chicago: University of Chicago Press.

Dudley, R. M. (1991). IQ and heredity [Letter to the editor]. *Science*, 252, 191.

Elkind, D. (1970). The origins of religion in the child. *Review of Religious Research*, 12, 35–42.

256

Francis, L. J., & Wilcox, C. (1996). Religion and gender orientation. *Personality and Individual Differences*, 20, 119–21.

Fullerton, J. T., & Hunsberger, B. (1982). A unidimensional measure of Christian Orthodoxy. *Journal for the Scientific Study of Religion*, 21, 317–26.

Goldman, R. (1964). *Religious thinking from childhood to adolescence*. New York: Seabury Press.

Hadaway, C. K. (1980). Denomination switching and religiosity. *Review of Religious Research*, 21, 451–61.

———. (1989). Identifying American apostates: A cluster analysis. *Journal for the Scientific Study of Religion*, 28, 201–15.

Hood, R. W., Jr., Spilka, B., Hunsberger, B., and Gorsuch, R. L. (1996). *The psychology of religion: An empirical approach*. New York: Guilford.

Hunsberger, B. (1976). Background religious denomination, parental emphasis, and the religious orientation of university students. *Journal for the Scientific Study of Religion*, 15, 251–55.

———. (1980). A reexamination of the antecedents of apostasy. *Review of Religious Research*, 21, 158–70.

———. (1983). Apostasy: A social learning perspective. *Review of Religious Research*, 25, 21–38.

———. (1985). Religion, age, life satisfaction, and perceived sources of religiousness: A Study of older persons. *Journal of Gerontology*, 40, 615–20.

———. (1985). Religion and prejudice: The role of religious fundamentalism, quest, and right-wing authoritarianism. *Journal of Social Issues*, 51, 113–29.

———. (1996). Religious fundamentalism, right-wing authoritarianism and hostility toward homosexuals in non-Christian religious groups. *International Journal for the Psychology of Religion*, 6, 39–49.

Hunsberger, B., Alisat, S., Pancer, S. M., and Pratt, M. (1996). Religious fundamentalism and religious doubts: Content, connections and complexity of thinking. *The International Journal for the Psychology of Religion*, 6, 201–20.

Hunsberger, B., & Brown, L. B. (1984). Religious socialization, apostasy, and the impact of family background. *Journal for the Scientific Study of Religion*, 23, 239–51.

Hunsberger, B., McKenzie, B., Pratt, M., and Pancer, S. M. (1993). Religious doubt: A social psychological analysis. *Research in the Social Scientific Study of Religion*, 5, 27–51.

Hunsberger, B., & Platonow, E. (1986). Religion and helping charitable causes. *Journal of Psychology*, 120, 517–28.

Hyde, K. E. (1990). *Religion in childhood and adolescence: A comprehensive review of the research.* Birmingham, Ala.: Religious Education Press.

James, W. (1902/1985). *The varieties of religious experience.* Cambridge, Mass.: Harvard University Press.

Jung, C. G. (1933). *Modern man in search of a soul* (W. S. Dell & C. F. Baynes, trans.). New York: Harcourt, Brace.

———. (1938). *Psychology and religion.* New Haven, Conn.: Yale University Press.

Kluegel, J. R. (1980). Denominational mobility: Current patterns and recent trends. *Journal for the Scientific Study of Religion*, 19, 26–39.

Kohlberg, L. (1980). Stages of moral development as a basis for moral education. In B. Munsey (Ed.), *Moral development, moral education, and Kohlberg* (pp. 15–98). Birmingham, Ala.: Religious Education Press.

Kotre, J. N. (1971). *The view from the border.* Chicago: Aldine/Atherton.

Leuba, J. H. (1896). A study in the psychology of religious phenomena. *American Journal of Psychology*, 7, 309–85.

Levin, J. S., Taylor, R. J., and Chatters, L. M. (1994). Race and gender differences in religiosity among older adults: Findings from four national surveys. *Journal of Gerontology: Social Sciences*, 49, S137–S145.

Nelsen, H. M. (1981). Religious conformity in an age of disbelief: Contextual effects of time, denomination, and family processes upon church decline and apostasy. *American Sociological Review*, 46, 632–40.

Nelsen, H. M., & Potvin, R. H. (1981). Gender and regional differences in the religiosity of Protestant adolescents. *Review of Religious Research*, 22, 268–85.

Ozorak, E. (1989). Social and cognitive influences on the development of religious beliefs and commitment in adolescence. *Journal for the Scientific Study of Religion*, 28, 448–63.

Paloutzian, R. F. (1996). *Invitation to the psychology of religion* (2nd ed.). Boston: Allyn & Bacon.

Piaget, J. (1952). *The origins of intelligence in children* (M. Cook, trans.). New York: International Universities Press. (Original work published 1936)

———. (1954). *The construction of reality in the child* (M. Cook, trans.). New York: Basic Books. (Original work published 1937).

Pratto, F., Sidanius, J., Stallworth, L. M., and Malle, T. F. (1994). Social dominance orientation: A personality variable predicting social and political attitudes. *Journal of Personality and Social Psychology*, 67, 741–63.

Richardson, J. T. (1985). The active vs. passive convert: Paradigm conflict in conversion/recruitment research. *Journal for the Scientific Study of Religion*, 24, 163–79.

Roof, W. C., & Hadaway, C. K. (1977). Shifts in religious preference—the mid-seventies. *Journal for the Scientific Study of Religion*, 16, 409–12.

Roof, W. C., & McKinney, W., Jr. (1987). *American mainline religion*. New Brunswick, N.J.: Rutgers University Press.

Thompson, E. H. (1991). Beneath the status characteristics: Gender variations in religiousness. *Journal for the Scientific Study of Religion*, 30, 381–94.

Waller, N. G., Kojetin, B. A., Bouchard, T. J., Jr., Lykken, D. T., and Tellegen, A. (1990). Genetic and environmental influences on religious interests, attitudes, and values: A study of twins reared apart and together. *Psychological Science, 1,* 138–42.

Wulff, D. M. (1991). *Psychology of religion: Classic and contemporary views.* New York: Wiley.

Wuthnow, R., & Mellinger, G. (1978). Religious loyalty, defection, and experimentation: A longitudinal analysis of university men. *Review of Religious Research, 19,* 231–45.

Wilson, J., & Sherkat, D. E. (1994). Returning to the fold. *Journal for the Scientific Study of Religion, 33,* 148–61.

Appendix A

Interview Schedule for Amazing Apostates

1. Gender

2. Age

3. Birth Order

4. Home Religion

5.(a) Was there a time when you were much *more* religious than you are now? Until when?

(b) Were you religiously *active*? Did you ever think you might have a "calling" to be a minister/priest? Go to a religious high school? Choir/youth group/etc?

6.(a) At what age did the *first questions* about your religion arise in your mind? When did you first begin to wonder if something was really true?

(b) (If necessary) Do you remember what the particular belief, or experience was?

7. Did you feel guilty or afraid about questioning your religion?

8.(a) Did you ask anyone, like your parents or a teacher/minister, for help in dealing with these questions?
    (b) What was their response?
    (c) Did this help? Why/why not?
    (d) Did you talk with anyone else, or read things, to help you decide?

9. (If relevant) Did your parents realize that your questions had not gone away?

10. Who *did* know about your questions?

11. What other things/questions came up that led you to change your religious beliefs? Were there other things/experiences?

12. Would you say now that you are still a _____ in terms of your religious beliefs?
    (If relevant) How old were you when you stopped considering yourself a _____ in terms of religious beliefs?

13. Do your parents/family realize now what your real religious views are?
    (If no) Who does?

14. Do you now feel any guilt or fear about your religious views?

15. Do you think it likely/unlikely that you will some day go back to your old beliefs?

16. Have you seen the movie *Back to the Future*? I would like to play a "back to the future" game with you. Suppose

that you were to meet yourself from XX years ago, that is, *before* you left your religion. I'll be the YY-year-old you, and you be the present you. Explain to your younger self (me) what has happened since (regarding religion) and why. Why don't you believe as much as you should?

What would be the reaction of the younger you?

17. Did you have other problems with your parents during the time you were dropping some of your religious beliefs? Were you having a "difficult time" then?

18. Almost everybody has questions about their religion while they are growing up, but they keep on believing. Very few are able to reject large parts (or all of it) as you did. What's the difference? What's different about you, compared, say, with your brother or sister?

19. What has your loss of faith cost you? In what ways are you sad because you no longer believe?

20. What have you gotten from it? In what ways are you glad because you no longer believe?

21. Now here's a tough question: Why not go back to the "bosom of Abraham"? Things would be so much simpler— your parents/family would be pleased; the world would be simpler, you would have the security of beliefs and a supportive church, and so on. Why not go back?

22. If you have children some day, how will you raise them? Will you give them a religious upbringing? Will you take/send them to church? Why/why not?

23. Now suppose a young person, say XX years old [S's doubting age] came to you for some advice. S/he had been

raised a Christian, and religion had played a big part in how s/he had been raised. But now this person is having questions about that religion (e.g., similar doubt to S: ethnocentrism of religion, Bible vs. evolution, problem of evil, danger of believing something because of faith, not reason . . .). And s/he wanted to know what s/he should do, and so came to you for advice. What would you say?

24. One more thing: How did you do in elementary and high school? (Grades?)

* * * *

That is the end of the questions I wanted to ask you. Your answers have been very interesting—you have obviously thought about this a lot. I really appreciate your willingness to be interviewed. Maybe there are some things you think I should have asked, but didn't, or something else you would like to tell me about how you arrived at your present position about religion, but didn't get the chance. Is there anything like that you would like to add?

Okay, that ends the interview itself, but I said earlier that you could ask me questions, if you like. Is there anything you would like to ask me?

Appendix B

Interview Schedule for Amazing Believers

1. Gender

2. Age

3. Birth Order

4. Home Religion
Explore further—e.g., grandparents?

5.(a) Was there a time when you were much *less* religious than you are now? Until when?

(b) Were you religiously *active* at all when you were younger? Go to church, SS, choir, church camp, youth group, religious high school?

(c) Were most of the kids you went to school with, say, religious? (If "yes") How did that make you feel, being unreligious?

6.(a) At what age did you *first* start to think that some religious teachings might be right, true?

(b) (If necessary) Do you remember what the particular belief, or experience was?

7. Did you feel guilty or afraid about becoming more religious?

8.(a) Did you ask anyone, like your parents or a teacher/minister, for help in dealing with your questions and emerging religious beliefs?

(b) What was their response?

(c) Did this help? Why/why not?

9. (If relevant) Did (your parents) realize that you continued to hold religious beliefs after talking with them?

10. Who *did* know about your emerging religious beliefs?

11. What other things came up that led you to become more religious?

Were there other things/experiences?

12. You said that you are now a _____ ? How old were you when you began to consider yourself a _____ in terms of religious beliefs?

(b) How religious are you now? (go to church, pray, read scripture, volunteer, organizations?)

13. Do your parents/family realize now what your real religious views are?

(If no) Who does?

14. Do you now feel any guilt or fear (or regret) about your religious views?

266

15. Do you think it likely/unlikely that you will some day go back to your old (nonreligious) beliefs?

16. Have you seen the movie *Back to the Future*? I would like to play a "back to the future" game with you. Suppose that you were to meet yourself from XX years ago, that is, *before* you became a _____ . I'll be the YY-year-old you, and you be the present you. Explain to your younger self (me) what has happened since (regarding religion) and why. Why did you become religious in spite of your nonreligious training?

What would be the reaction of the younger you?

17. Did you have any other problems with your parents during the time you were becoming more religious? Were you having a "difficult time" then?

18. (If necessary) Almost everybody who grows up (in a nonreligious home) continues to be nonreligious later. Very few are able to reject large parts of their nonreligious background as you did. What's the difference? What's different about you, compared, say, with your brother or sister?

19. What has your turn to religion cost you? In what ways are you sad/sorry about becoming religious?

20. What have you gotten from it? In what ways are you glad that you became religious?

21. Now here's a tough question: Why not go back to the nonreligious beliefs of your family? Your parents/family would be pleased. Church wouldn't complicate your life (no time commitment, etc.). Why not go back?

22. If you have children some day, how will you raise them? Will you give them a religious upbringing? Will you take/send them to church? Why/why not?

23. Now suppose a young person, say XX years old [S's emerging religion age] came to you for some advice. S/he had been raised in a nonreligious family, but now this person is thinking about becoming much more religious. And s/he wanted to know what s/he should do, and so came to you for advice. What would you say?

24. One more thing: How did you do in elementary and high school? (grades?)

25. And finally, can you, offhand, tell me what the Ten Commandments are?

*   *   *   *

That is the end of the questions I wanted to ask you. Your answers have been very interesting—you have obviously thought about this a lot. I really appreciate your willingness to be interviewed. Maybe there are some things you think I should have asked, but didn't, or something else you would like to tell me about how you arrived at your present position about religion, but didn't get the chance. Is there anything like that you would like to add?

Okay, that ends the interview itself—is there anything about the study you would like to know now?